To Marjory.
from.
Pauline & al.
X 92

Have a merry Christmas
with your family.

HOLIDAY SCRAP CRAFTS

Marti Michell

MEREDITH® PRESS

New York

Dear Scrap Crafter,

For nearly 20 years, crafters have benefitted from the prolific design talent of Marti Michell. The books, patterns, kits, and gadgets that are the products of her imagination have encouraged thousands of casual sewing hobbyists to embark on a journey of discovery in fabric crafts.

   Meredith® Press is proud to bring you Marti's latest ideas for holiday crafting. With her usual flair for the witty and whimsical, Marti unveils delightful new projects for popular holidays, as well as tips and ideas for any-occasion crafting. With 44 big color photos, step-by-step directions, and Ann Nunemacher's wonderful illustrations, *Holiday Scrap Crafts* is brimming with ideas for holiday decorating and gift-giving. This is every fabric lover's idea of fun.

Sincerely,
Patricia Wilens
Editorial Project Manager

ACKNOWLEDGMENTS

The list of names below is not just a list of names. It is the roll call of a wonderful support team that really made this book possible. I can never fully express my grateful appreciation to each of them.

Marti Michell

Meredith® Press is an imprint of Meredith® Books:
President, Book Group: Joseph J. Ward
Vice President, Editorial Director: Elizabeth P. Rice

For Meredith® Press:
Executive Editor: Connie Schrader
Editorial Project Manager: Patricia Wilens
Production Manager: Bill Rose
Book Designer: Ulrich Ruchti
Illustrations: Ann Davis Nunemacher
Photography: Bread and Butter Studio, Atlanta, Georgia
Photo Stylings: Marti Michell, Stacy Michell
Quilter's Ink Associates: Ann Cookston, Sally Cutler, Martha
   Dudley, Narda Dudley, Jenny Lynn Price, Camellia Pesto

ISBN: 0-696-02358-X
Library of Congress Catalog Card Number: 91-052556

Printed in the United States of America
10   9   8   7   6   5   4   3   2   1

INTRODUCTION

This is the third book I have written for Meredith Press on scrap projects. Some people might think I'm in a rut, but don't worry, I just love this subject. If you are familiar with the first two books, *Country Fabric Scrap Crafts* and *Scrap Patchwork and Quilting*, you will recognize similarities in this book.

Holiday Scrap Crafts features fabric craft items for holiday enjoyment that favor the country look and quilting techniques. There is a reason. These days, many of us have more quilting fabrics than garment fabrics in our scrap bags. I definitely do; the fabrics for all three books came from my own fabric/scrap collection. These designs, however, are very adaptable to other materials.

I hope you will start with these ideas, but make the projects your own through personal fabric decisions, unique or collected trims, and variations. You may think you don't want to make decisions or that you can't put colors together. Please, humor me and give it a try. You may like it, it can't hurt, and I'll feel better.

It is especially easy for you to indulge me with these scrap projects. The holidays featured in this book generally have traditional color themes that I chose to honor, but that doesn't mean you have to! Some projects, interpreted in another color, wouldn't be restricted to holiday use at all.

Your scrap projects will look different from mine, because they will reflect your taste in fabrics collected over the years. That is one of the things that will make them special.

Everyone involved in this project has worked hard to create a book you will value. It is well illustrated and full of color photographs. You will get lots of information even if all you do is "read" the pictures.

I hope, however, that you will also read the words. Even if you aren't making a particular project, you may want to scan the headings throughout the book. Some of the best techniques and tidbits are in the how-to sections. In addition to scrap projects, easy and efficient techniques are another passion of mine. I try to include them in my instructions in the hope that you will like them enough to make them part of your own standard procedures.

Occasionally it will be necessary to refer to another project for procedures that are repetitive. Hopefully, the extra projects we are able to include in the book by eliminating repetition will be worth any inconvenience this might cause.

One good project seems to make us think of another and there are always ideas that won't fit in the book. Because the best thing to do with ideas is share them, you will find some sketches and ideas for variations sprinkled through the book.

CONTENTS

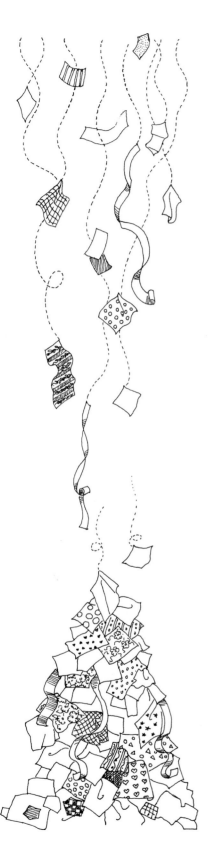

CHAPTER ONE

UNDERSTANDING SCRAPS AND COLLECTING THEM

Why Are Scrap Projects So Popular?

Recycling

Saving and using fabric scraps was the original recycling program. The Puritan ethic and the "Clean Plate Club" have historically encouraged us to make something from nothing, supporting an attitude that it is wasteful to throw anything away. "Use it up, wear it out, make it do, or do without" was the philosophy many of us grew up with or heard from our grandparents.

Mind Games

Self-satisfaction is one of the greatest emotions realized by making scrap projects. Anyone who has ever rolled and saved and moved fabric scraps saying, "Someday, I'm going to want that," will recognize the triumphant, smug feeling that results when the scraps are actually used.

Combined with the hoarding instinct some of us have about fabric, it's simple—we *have* to make scrap projects.

Using scraps is also a great psychological release. At some point, each of us will say, "I can't buy another piece of fabric until I use what I have." This expression verbalizes our collective guilt. Using some of that fabric is a great release for me, because it frees me to buy more.

Memories

Scraps often hold special memories. Sometimes those memories are associated with a special garment, but more and more it can be a fabric left from a favorite quilt. Sometimes the attachment to the fabric itself is great, and finding another way to use it is wonderful.

Many of my fabrics are not really leftover, but being cut into for the first time. It's almost embarrassing to admit that I still attach the enjoyment of the moment of acquisition to most of my fabrics. Special stores, trips, trades, gifts from friends are all pleasant memories associated with these projects.

Loving and Collecting Fabrics

Loving and collecting textiles is enough to get some people into making scrap projects. Fabric is now very available and affluence more prevalent, so there are many of us now who have great accumulations of fabric. It is not known when the first official fabric collection was begun, but it is thought that the 1980s and 1990s will go down in textile history as decades when many prominent fabric collections developed and perhaps fabric collectors achieved a certain status.

For the fabric collector, scrap quilts and scrap projects provide a twofold attraction—the reason to have so many fabrics and the way to use them.

Scrap Quilts

Many people think scrap quilts will be the most popular style of quilts in the 1990s. That popularity will influence the design of smaller projects. While most of the quilt projects in this book are quite small, if you have lots of fabric and need bigger projects, see *Scrap Patchwork and Quilting*, also published by Meredith Press. At one time, scrap quilts had a hand-me-down feeling associated with someone financially unable to buy matching fabric. That way of thinking has changed; today's scrap quilts are more likely to be a symbol of affluence. Modern scrap quilts often represent hours of shopping and a great personal collection of fabrics bought "just in case." A scrap quilt is a great way to showcase a fabric collection.

Understanding Your Scraps

In the purest sense of the word, it seems that scrap projects should be made from fabric left over after cutting out a garment or a quilt, or recycled from salvageable sections of a used-up garment. My interpretation of scrap is much broader. I feel that *any* fabric I haven't used yet is "leftover" or "scrap" fabric.

Another of my ideas about scrap projects is that they don't just use small quantities of fabric, but that they may use many different fabrics together. Even people who love the look of scrap projects find putting them together is an acquired skill. It hasn't been very long since we even began to put coordinating prints together. The key word there is *coordinating*, because freethinking combinations like a plaid with a floral were not highly regarded until recently. The point is that putting lots of prints together is difficult for most people.

Personally, I think the most common mistake in combining prints is overmatching. It's boring. Working with scraps is a great opportunity to stretch your range of combinations.

Consider the Color

Sort through your scraps, separating them by color families. You'll probably discover some piles are overflowing and that you want to subdivide them by shade or by pattern.

You may find that you don't own any scraps of some colors. That will mean that you are working with a limited palette.

Consider the Fiber

Compatibility of fibers is very important in many of these projects. Actual compatibility needs in the sewing process must be met as well as those demanded for dry cleaning or laundry. When working with scraps, it may be difficult to know the care requirements of an individual fabric. If in doubt about the washability of any material, test it before including it in a project that will require washing.

Consider the Rest

It is important to think of fabrics in more ways than color or fiber. Learn to look for pleasing contrasts. There are different ways to use contrast as a design tool. This is not just contrast in hue, but contrast in light and dark, random or rigid, small or large motifs, calm or busy. Look at your fabrics and pick some of each. Stand back at least 6 feet and see if your choices look different from that vantage point.

The mood you are trying to create may be the deciding factor in whether a questionable fabric should be used.

Use the designs in this book and others as inspiration. No matter how much you love something you see, it is unrealistic to try to duplicate exactly the same fabrics and colors.

How Much Fabric Do I Need?

This seems to be the first question a sewer asks. Because these projects really are designed to be made from scraps, only specific measurements over ¼ yard are listed. If you are using very small scraps, lay them over the patterns to see if you have enough. All fabric requirements given in yards refer to fabrics that are 45 inches wide.

Don't Worry, I Have Enough Fabric!

Of course, no one can define enough. As one of my friends says, "You can never be too thin, too rich, or have too much fabric." Many of you are reading this because you already have lots of fabric and I'm sure at one time or another you have felt guilty about your purchases.

Organize a fabric exchange. This works on the same principle as a cookie exchange. Just as it is easier for one person to make 10 dozen of the same cookie than a half dozen each of 20 cookies, it is easier for each person to bring a big piece of fabric, or 80 matching triangles, to the exchange.

Be creative. Many prints are very attractive on the wrong side, especially if you want the look of muted, old-looking fabrics.

Dyeing old fabrics to make them coordinate is a good way to make scraps more useful. The two most common ways of changing fabric color are tea dyeing and overdyeing.

Tea dyeing is very popular right now and is just what it says, using tea to change the fabric color. It makes fabric seem aged and is often used to give fabric a stained, primitive look. I sometimes tea-dye small craft projects, but I am reticent to tea-dye fabric for a quilt that I expect to wash and/or keep a long time. Tea stains gradually wash out, and we don't know the long-term effects of the acids in tea on the fabric. Colors available with tea and coffee are limited and, if you want to dye much yardage, you can't be very exacting with repeat attempts.

Metric Conversion
1 Meter = 39.37 inches
1 inch = 2.54 cms
Yards × .9144 = meters
Inches × 2.54 = cms

Overdyeing gives more controllable results and has the advantage of a wide range of color choices. Best results will be achieved with cold-water fiber-reactive dyes on 100 percent cotton fabrics. The readily available all-purpose dye is not permanent enough for a long lasting quilt.

Painting fabric is currently the rage. Craft and fabric stores have large selections of permanent fabric paints and dyes that are applied with a brush or tip applicator. These can be used to create greater variety in the fabrics you have. Read the instructions carefully and test a scrap before using the paint on a new fabric for a quilt or project that you plan to wash or use for a long time.

Buy creatively. Buying carefully in remnant bins and at sales, even garage sales, will help you to develop a broader variety of scraps.

Accept gifts. Let people know you enjoy using scraps—you'll be amazed at how much fabric will be given to you. Don't feel guilty, either, because the givers have relieved themselves of responsibility for *using* the fabric. Be discriminating—eliminate fabrics you feel are unsuitable right away; otherwise your house may be completely taken over with fabric.

CHAPTER TWO

GETTING DOWN TO BUSINESS

General Procedures

This chapter covers basic information on techniques, tools, and procedures so I can have room for full-size patterns and more projects by avoiding repetition. Whenever you feel project instructions aren't thorough enough, refer back to this chapter for basic information.

Studio Space

No matter how much or how little space you have, calling it your studio immediately elevates your work to a higher plane. Never mind if it was the kitchen table moments ago, it is now the area you are using for a creative process and is more appropriately called a studio.

Tools

General. If you have done much sewing or quilting recently, most of the tools you need are probably already among your sewing supplies: good scissors (large and small), a seam ripper, thimble, needles and thread, marking tools, pins, and rulers. A steam iron and ironing board are essential.

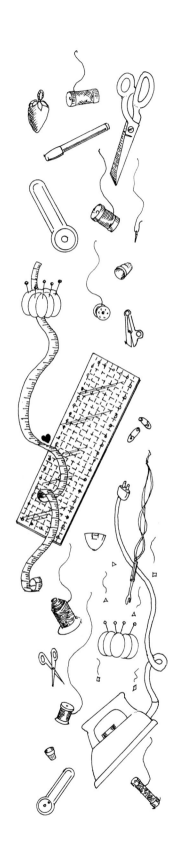

Sewing machine. Nearly all the projects require some sewing that is best done with a sewing machine. It doesn't need to be fancy, just so it stitches forward; backstitching is nice and zigzag stitching is used on a few projects.

If you haven't used your machine in a while, dust it off, oil it, clean out the lint, and put in a new needle (size 14/90). Even if the needle isn't bent, if you don't remember when you changed it last, it's probably too dull to use.

The tension must be properly adjusted. If it isn't, you may get puckered seams (tension too tight) or fabrics may pull apart and stitches will show on the right side (tension too loose). Read your owner's manual for help in making adjustments.

A design wall. One tool you may not already have is a design wall. It sounds sophisticated, but it can be as elaborate or as simple as your space and budget allow. The ultimate would be an entire wall of your studio covered with felt or bulletin board material, so you can position fabrics and stand back to study the effect. Most people, however, use a large bulletin board or a piece of felt wrapped around a 3 × 4-foot board of plastic foam.

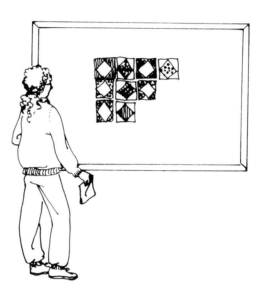

Using the Patterns in This Book

Tracing patterns. In this book, it was necessary to divide patterns that exceed the page size. If any pattern says "Part A" or "Part B," make sure you find the second piece and match the connecting edges to complete the tracing to make one full-size pattern.

Enlarging patterns. Some patterns are printed on a grid. The easiest way to enlarge a pattern from the grid is to visit your local photocopy shop and let a machine do it for you. Many photocopy machines now have an enlargement feature, so all you have to do is keep enlarging successive copies until the grid squares are the desired size. With this method, you may have to be happy with a somewhat approximate finished size, but most times you will be able to come fairly close.

The alternative is to do the work yourself, using a ruler, pencil, eraser, and a large piece of paper. First, duplicate the grid on your paper, drawing whatever size squares are required. Make sure you have the right number of squares both vertically and horizontally. Next, your task is to duplicate the image inside each square on the full-size grid. Be sure to keep the arrangement and proportions within each square the same as on the small grid. This is not really a difficult task, just a time-consuming one.

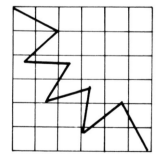

ENLARGING

Grainline designation. Unless patterns are to be placed on the fold, they contain a grainline arrow. Whenever possible, align this arrow with the lengthwise grain (parallel to the selvage). Second choice is for the arrow to be going with the crosswise grain, perpendicular to the lengthwise grain.

The selvage is often missing from scrap fabrics. Determine the direction of the lengthwise grain by pulling on opposite sides of the scrap in the same direction as the threads run. The direction that has the least stretch is the lengthwise grain.

When patterns say "Place on fold," then the fold of the fabric should be made on the lengthwise grain.

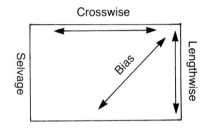

Bias. Bias refers to cutting across the grainline at any angle. True bias cuts at a 45-degree angle, which creates an edge with a great deal of stretch. Bias can be the greatest pest or the best assistance, depending on the technique. Most things are cut on the straight of the grain and bias is saved for special purposes.

Preparing Scraps for Use

Press. Scraps almost always need to be pressed to assure accurate cutting.

Preshrink. Fabrics for place mats, napkins, and other items that will be washed regularly should be preshrunk.

Preshrink, maybe. For projects that will seldom or never be washed, such as scrap wreaths, preshrinking is not so vital.

First, understand that I belong to the camp that does not automatically preshrink every fabric. I know people who say (with an air of superiority, I might add) that they never walk in the door with fabric without stopping at the washing machine to preshrink it. I don't know if people really *do* that, but I do know people who *say* that. If you are someone who really does this, a big bonus is that your scraps are already preshrunk and you can skip the next few paragraphs.

There are several reasons that I don't routinely preshrink. I have a lot of unused fabric and if, by chance, it stays that way, then I won't have spent a lot of time shrinking fabric for the sake of shrinking. Frankly, that isn't on the list of things I do for fun.

In addition, I mostly piece and quilt by machine, so I like the crisp hand of finished goods straight from the store. I feel they are easier to piece and quilt by machine. The crisp hand is lost in the first wash if you use hot water, detergent, and double rinses. I want to point out, however, that my friends who do a lot of hand quilting say it is easier on their joints to remove that crispness.

Also, I find the look of unwashed fabrics more appealing. It may be some time before a project is washed, so I want to maintain that new look as long as possible.

I do test fabrics for shrinkage and colorfastness when I'm making quilts. But because I am using known fabrics and small pieces, I admit to being a gambler in many scrap craft projects. I don't even test little pieces.

How to preshrink. If you preshrink, I would like to recommend the following procedures.

For little projects, the solution is simple. The fabric pieces are usually small and wrinkled. Simply run hot water over the fabrics until they are saturated, then iron them dry. This is perfect shrinking because it is heat on wet fibers that causes shrinking.

For larger projects, cut a piece of fabric slightly larger than what you need for the project. Put similar colors together and put them in the last rinse cycle on your washing machine. Use cold water. Then dry the fabrics in the dryer, but don't over dry. Press each piece with a steam iron. If any fabric is unusually limp, spray it with sizing (not starch) when you press. It is not necessary to use soap or detergent as they do not promote shrinkage, but only facilitate color fading. It is not necessary to use hot water in the washing machine. Remember, it is heat on the wet fibers that causes shrinkage, and the dryer will do that fine.

The fallacy in this method is that it doesn't give you an opportunity to look at each fabric for colorfastness. If you are not familiar with the fabrics, you can dip a corner of each one into warm water in a large, clear bowl; squeeze out the water, looking for any telltale bleeding of color. Lay aside questionable fabrics and retest. It may be necessary to wash these fabrics separately until there is no sign of bleeding or running color.

Cutting

Scissors. If using scissors, make sure they are sharp. Keep materials as flat as possible during cutting to prevent distortion. When cutting multiple layers of fabric from the same pattern, pin the layers together to prevent slippage.

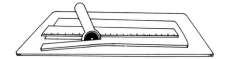

Rotary cutting method. The rotary cutter is a tool that looks and operates like a pizza cutter, but it is used in sewing, quilting, and crafts circles for cutting fabrics, particularly long, straight cuts. The cutter is very sharp, so it requires a special mat for cutting on to protect both the cutting surface and the blade. In most cases, a thick acrylic ruler completes the set, providing a straight, hard edge to guide the blade. A rotary cutter is more accurate than scissors because all cutting is done with the fabrics flat. Everything in this book can be made with scissors, but rotary cutting makes so many things both easier and more accurate that you should consider it.

"Cut 2." In sewing jargon, "Cut 2" means that you fold one layer of fabric with either right sides or wrong sides together, put the pattern on top, and cut two layers of fabric at once. This process ensures having both a left section and a right section for pieces that must be cut in a mirror image, such as vest fronts.

If your scrap isn't big enough to fold, it may be necessary to make two separate cuttings. Cut with the pattern right side up for one piece and right side down for the other.

Rough cut. When it is appropriate to cut the *approximate* size, allowing for seams instead of cutting exactly on a drawn line, we call it rough cut. This usually means we are *sewing* exactly on a drawn line and will trim the seam allowances after sewing.

Marking

Transferring markings from patterns to fabric is often a crucial step in the success of a project. Making sure marks are easily removable is also important.

The actual marking process is easiest when tracing from the pattern to the fabric on a light table. Small portable versions are readily available for crafts-oriented people. A glass tabletop with a light placed under it is a good improvised version.

Old standbys for marking include tracing wheel and paper, tailor's chalk, clipping into the seam line, or notching out. Newer tools are the water-erasable marker and evaporating marker. Each has a place and generally comes with good instructions. The important points are don't skip marking and test your marking method on scraps before marking the fabric you intend to use.

The Actual Sewing

Thread. Use good-quality thread; cheap threads break and cause lint build-up in your machine. Take time to learn about the wonderful metallic threads and lustrous rayons that can give special finishing details to projects. For machine quilting, try the fine transparent nylon thread (commonly called "invisible") in the top threading position with regular thread in the bobbin.

Seam allowances. The seam allowance generally allowed is ¼ inch. If you are accustomed to garment sewing and new to craft sewing and patchwork, this might seem tiny compared to the ⅝-inch seam allowance customary for garments. Many sewing machines have a presser foot with a toe ¼ inch wide. Until you become comfortable eye balling the measurement, it may be worth it to mark some of the seam allowances.

No seam allowance. Sometimes there is no seam allowance on the patterns. This means the line given is the sewing line, not the cutting line. Patterns are given this way when the shaping of the item depends on accurate sewing. It is much easier to sew directly on a drawn line than to cut something with a ¼-inch seam allowance and then sew a consistent ¼ inch from the cut edge. See Line and Turn in this chapter for a more complete explanation of this process.

Right sides together. Unless otherwise stated, all seams are made with the right sides of the two pieces touching.

Clipping

Clipping is when sharp-pointed scissors are used to carefully cut into the seam allowance so it will spread or overlap without wrinkles when it is

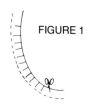

FIGURE 1

FIGURE 2

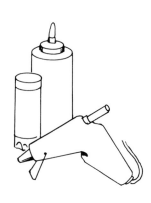

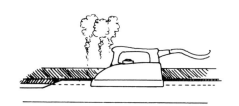

turned inside the stitched items. Clipping is necessary on all curved areas.

On inside curves, clipping allows the seam allowances to spread when turned (Figure 1). On outside curves, notching is best as it prevents seam allowances from piling up and rippling when turned (Figure 2). The more curved a seam, the more clipping is needed. Sharp changes in direction also must be clipped.

Gluing and Fusing

Sometimes the best "stitch" is a hot-glue gun or fabric glue. This does not mean all-purpose white glue, which is great for many things but makes most fabrics very stiff. Check your fabric store for glues especially designed to be used with fabric. Hot glue can be messy, frustrating, and worse, but it is sometimes the only solution, the fastest, and the most secure.

Glue sticks are another convenient item often used for holding fabric temporarily in position. The adhesive washes out, but provides basting without the time of sewing and without the surface distortion of pins.

Gluing and fusing are messier than sewing techniques and, if the adhesives end up in the wrong place, can be frustrating. Make sure you have a cleared work surface that is properly protected. Have a damp cloth for wiping up drops and spills of water-soluble glues immediately.

Fusibles are discussed more thoroughly under Appliqué Techniques (page 17). There are cleaning agents for iron surfaces that have met the wrong side of the fusibles, but being careful is easier. Putting scrap fabric on the ironing board when using fusibles saves lots of ironing board covers.

Painting

Painting can replace stitching in some decorative areas. There are wonderful textile paints available, some with applicator points (no brush needed), so think about those possibilities if painting appeals to you more than zigzag stitching.

Pressing

Pressing is not an option—it is a very important step in successful projects. Try to press a seam before you sew across it; sometimes careful and firm "finger pressing" can postpone that for one step, but use this practice judiciously.

Patchwork seam allowances are usually pressed in the same direction, not open as in dressmaking. They are pressed towards the darker fabric unless there is an overriding reason. Press both seams in the same direction in craft items that are going to be stuffed, too.

Steam irons can be very powerful, so make sure you don't use a hard distorting action with your iron.

Specific Techniques

Appliqué Techniques

Quick and easy fused appliqué. This appliqué technique incorporates making the design fabric fusible by ironing a paper-backed fusible web to the wrong side of the fabric. In the past, fused fabrics were synonymous with *stiff* and, having done it once, lots of people rejected the concept. While the new fusing materials add some stiffness, it is very minimal. So if you haven't tried fusing recently, you might want to now.

Stitch Witchery™, a fusing product that is fine for many things, is not suitable for this fused appliqué technique because it lacks the paper protective shield.

1. Paper backing allows you to draw or trace the original design on the paper (Figure 1). But remember—if the design is not symmetrical, it will be reversed when the fabric is turned over and pressed in place later.

2. Follow manufacturer's instructions to fuse the paper-backed web to the back of the fabric. This fusing process converts regular fabric to fusible fabric. Cut the desired shape on the drawn line (Figure 2).

3. Remove the paper backing (Figure 3), then turn the piece over and iron it in place on the appliqué background fabric (Figure 4).

4. It is optional, but desirable to finish the edge of the appliqué. Textile paints are popular and give a nice outline of color. Or, use a narrow, relatively close zigzag stitch to cover the cut edges. Use invisible thread in the sewing machine needle with regular thread in the bobbin or regular sewing thread in both positions. When the thread is visible, however, your stitch must be more carefully made (Figure 5).

Another finishing option is a decorative stitch of hand embroidery or from your sewing machine (especially if you are lucky enough to have a machine that does a stitch that looks like a featherstitch or buttonhole stitch). For this, use a contrasting thread color.

Easy, but not quick appliqué. This technique incorporates freezer paper for ease and accuracy and is as quick as any hand appliqué.

1. Cut freezer paper the exact size of the appliqué design.

2. Rough-cut fabric to approximately the size of the design, adding a ³/₁₆-inch seam allowance.

3. Center the freezer paper on the fabric with the unwaxed surface of paper touching the wrong side of the fabric.

4. With the tip of the iron, press the edge of the fabric over the edge of the paper. The fabric will stick slightly to the waxy surface, but it doesn't make your iron sticky (Figure 6).

5. Position the appliqué on the background fabric; hand-sew it in place with a hidden stitch that just catches the edge of the appliqué (Figure 7).

6. Remove the freezer paper as you approach the starting point, or stitch all the way around, then cut away the background fabric from behind the appliqué and slip the paper out.

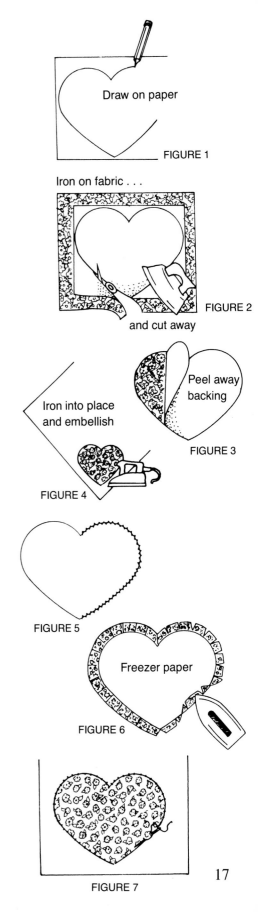

Draw on paper

FIGURE 1

Iron on fabric . . .

FIGURE 2

and cut away

Peel away backing

FIGURE 3

Iron into place and embellish

FIGURE 4

FIGURE 5

Freezer paper

FIGURE 6

FIGURE 7

Line and turn appliqué. For a third appliqué method, see Line and Turn for Appliqué, page 21.

Patchwork

Patchwork is the process of piecing or sewing together with a seam multiple pieces of fabric to create a surface design that is usually, but not always, geometric in appearance.

Quilting

Quilting is the process of stitching together three layers of materials—a top, a bottom (or backing), and a quilt batting. First, the layers must be secured together by basting or, my preference, pin basting with safety pins.

Hand quilting is a simple running stitch. While champion quilters can take 12 to 15 stitches per inch (that's visible stitches on top of the quilt), 10 to 12 stitches per inch is considered very good and 8 stitches per inch is a realistic goal. Consistent size is generally considered as important as tiny stitches. Most people use quilting thread and size 10 or 12 needles called *betweens* (quilting needles).

Knot a single strand of quilting thread. Insert the threaded needle through the quilt from the back; tug to pull the knot through the backing and hide it in the batting. Instead of knotting the thread, you can sometimes secure it in a seam allowance at the edge of your work.

Machine quilting is much faster, but not necessarily easier. My favorite way to machine quilt a multicolored quilt is with fine nylon invisible thread in the needle, and a cotton thread that matches the backing in the bobbin. Use 8 to 10 stitches per inch. It is usually necessary to loosen the upper tension. If you have trouble with layers bunching, make sure the presser foot pressure is not too hard. With a solid-colored quilt, matching cotton thread top and bottom is nice.

Batting is the soft material sandwiched between a quilt top and the back to give a quilt dimension and warmth. Polyester batting is the most commonly used today, because it is light, washes easily, and does not require as much quilting as cotton batting. Cotton batting, however, is making a strong comeback as new brands appear that are more suited to modern quilters. For most projects in this book, a medium-loft, bonded polyester batting is the best choice. If you have a brand you love, great; if not, here are a few tips on a complex subject.

There are typically three weights of polyester batting. Different brands use different identifying terms. The medium or average batt previously mentioned is used for most things. Low-loft is used when you want very little puffiness, as in garments or place mats. Thick batting is used for comforters.

Fleece is the generic name for a product sold in the interfacing section of fabric stores. I use it as a substitute for low-loft batting. For example, I would use it to line pillows I'm not going to quilt, but will stuff. It prevents lumps from showing through and produces a nice, smooth surface.

See Recommended Products on page 168.

Stuffing

Stuffing, the verb. An important stuffing technique is not to stuff too much at one time. Many smaller insertions are usually better than a few large ones. There are also degrees of stuffing, similar to degrees of doneness in cooking meat. Sometimes stuffing tools are needed. Crochet hooks, chop sticks, and wooden skewers—long, thin tools without sharp, damaging points—can be helpful for pushing stuffing into small places.

Stuff lightly when you want a little dimension in an area that will not get heavy use that tends to pack down the stuffing. It is also the way you stuff if you want to be able to bend the section in question.

Stuff firmly if the stuffing must stand up to wear and does not bend easily. Most pillows are stuffed firmly.

Stuff very firmly when you don't want any bend, such as in a doll or giraffe's neck.

Stuffing, the noun. Stuffing, loose fill, and polyester filling are words that might be used to describe the same thing. While there are other fillings, such as cotton, kapok, and foam, I recommend polyester for the projects in this book.

There are different kinds of polyester. Beware of loss-leader fiberfill that lays like a brick in one corner of a pillow. It is *not* a bargain. Price per ounce or pound or bag is not the determining factor for value. Price per volume filled is the first criterion for judging a good value. The second criterion is the feel of the product. You might call it the Fill-and-Feel Test. Before buying, compare how much volume the different stuffings fill. Think about how it feels through the bag when you squeeze it. In use, you want a filling that does not mat down and can be washed in the finished item.

Embroidery Stitches

Embroidery can add interesting detail, but few stitches are required to finish the projects in this book. They are illustrated below.

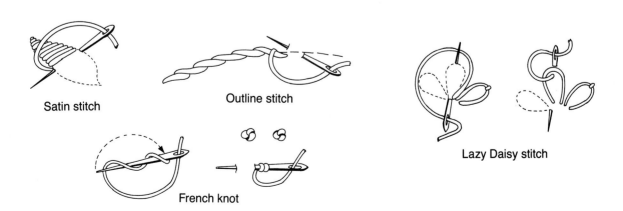

Satin stitch

Outline stitch

French knot

Lazy Daisy stitch

Fringe Techniques

Many of the items in this book take advantage of the old decorative technique of fringing fabric edges. With most fabrics except burlap, the fringe is more attractive if the fabric is first torn and has irregular edges than if it is cut. For our Chick Plant Stake (page 114), for example, the fabric was torn into short strips for each neck band.

To fringe, pull two or three horizontal threads from the fabric edge at a time. Keeping a little tension on the strip seems to make the threads pull more easily. Burlap must be cut into strips before fringing; however, after fringing, cutting the fringe in a jagged manner can give it a more natural appearance (see Scarecrow's clothes, page 128).

It is easier to fringe short pieces of fabric. If you are fringing a long edge, make the fringing area shorter by clipping perpendicularly across the number of threads you intend to fringe every 12 to 15 inches. Be very careful not to cut into the remaining fabric.

Line and Turn

Line and turn is a technique that makes easy work of small or detailed shapes that are to be stuffed or appliquéd. The patterns in this book that are appropriate for this technique *do not* include seam allowances. These shapes are cut out *after* they are sewn. Most people can stitch more accurately sewing directly on a drawn seam line than trying to stitch ¼ inch from the cut edge. And, when working with small or detailed shapes, the accuracy of stitching on a drawn seam line is crucial in determining the final shape. This method gives results well worth a little extra effort.

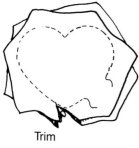

Trim

FIGURE 1

1. Rough-cut (see definition on page 15) if working with large pieces of fabric. Trace as many shapes as needed on the *wrong* side of the chosen fabric. Leave ½ inch between any two lines. Match the design fabric with its backing fabric, right sides together.

2. Using a small sewing machine stitch (12 to 14 stitches per inch) on very detailed shapes, stitch exactly on the line. An open-toed presser foot or clear presser foot makes it easier to see the sewing line and accurately guide the fabric.

3. Leave an opening in the seam for turning the lined piece inside out (Figure 1).

4. Trim and clip. See Clipping, page 15, for more details.

5. Turn carefully. When turning inside out, pay careful attention to detail areas. Use a small, dull-pointed item (such as chopsticks or a crochet hook) to prod points and corners to the maximum. Press judiciously; if an item is to be stuffed, pressing is sometimes omitted to avoid pressing in unsightly hard lines.

6. See Stuffing, page 19. If an item is stuffed after turning, push small amounts of filling into extremities first. Use the same poking tools to prod the stuffing into the extremities, then fill central areas. When satisfied, close openings.

7. Close opening. It is difficult to maintain a design line when you hand-sew the opening left in a seam for turning. If the item is exposed on both sides, however, there is little choice; use the least conspicuous small stitch to close a seam opening securely.

Rough Opening/Line and Turn for Appliqué

For items that have one side that never shows, there is another method. It is especially nice for appliqués. Cut two of the appliqué shape. Cut a slit in the back piece; with right sides together, stitch completely around the item. Then trim, clip, and turn the piece through the slit (Figure 2). Press, and you are ready to appliqué. Stuff the piece first for dimension when desired. Whip-stitch the slit shut if you think it necessary.

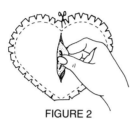

FIGURE 2

Finished Opening

This method is suitable for slightly exposed backs and hidden backs made by neatness fanatics. If you just can't accept a slit that is whipped shut, make a back section with a finished slit by seaming two pieces partially from each end. Leave the center open and press the seam allowances open (Figure 3). Now you have an opening that can be neatly sewn shut by hand.

See Flat-Edged Place Mats, page 25, for a Line and Turn variation that incorporates fusible fleece.

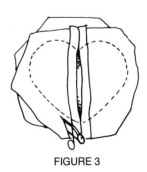

FIGURE 3

Pillow Finishing and Ruffles

See Starry Night Pillows, pages 61–65.

Stitch and Flip Technique

This is a process where fabrics are placed right sides together on a base or background square, often including quilt batting, and stitched together through all layers. Then the top layer is pressed open and the process is repeated.

String quilting is the traditional name often used to describe a stitch and flip process without batting and backing. It has come to imply the use of irregular scrap fabrics. In the past, it was common for patchworkers to cut shapes out of newspaper—diamonds or hexagons, for example—and then stitch and flip irregular scraps on it until the paper was covered (Figures 1, 2 and 3). They used a paper diamond as a pattern, trimmed the edges, and joined the diamonds for a wonderful Eight-Pointed Star (Figure 4).

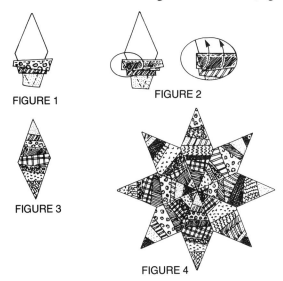

FIGURE 1

FIGURE 2

FIGURE 3

FIGURE 4

You can do the same thing with other shapes. Or, you can sew fabric scraps together until the new piece is big enough to cut out the heart or teddy bear or patchwork pieces you want.

String quilting is a great loosening up exercise to help people relax about putting odd fabrics together. It's fast, fun, effective, and very scrap conducive. Almost any item in this book can be made from string-quilted fabric.

Quilt-as-you-sew is another name associated with this process, but only if the stitching goes through batting and backing fabric at the same time as the pieced fabrics.

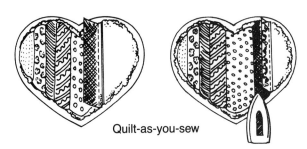

Quilt-as-you-sew

CHAPTER THREE

HOLIDAY FABRICS

Holiday print fabrics are the most helpful things ever invented for the person intent on holiday decorating. Whether you are working with scraps of holiday prints or other yardage from your fabric collection, the pressure for specific holiday projects is lessened by the fabric. For example, *any-thing* you make with a shamrock print reads "Irish."

Holiday-oriented fabric is available for each of the seven holidays featured in this book. But, rather than be restricted to what is available in a single year, I stockpile some each year for greater variety.

Because so many holiday events center around eating, it seems appropriate to include a few generic place mat and napkin-making instructions. Make them from appropriate holiday prints and they are no longer generic.

Flat-Edged Place Mats

If you have ever made quilted place mats, you know that the extra layer of quilt batting sewn into a seam can create a bump on the place mat edge. When someone sets a glass down on the edge, it might tip over and spill. This "no bumpy seam" technique for flat-edged place mats eliminates that problem.

Preshrink fabrics for place mats.

1. Cut paper-backed fusible webbing slightly larger than the finished rectangle (or other shape) desired. Fuse it to polyester fleece. On the paper side of the webbing, mark the finished design or size. Following the drawn line, cut the fusible fleece to the exact finished size or shape of the place mat.

For the Poinsettia place mats shown at left, a 14 × 18-inch rectangle was drawn (Figure 1). For rounded corners, use the pattern below.

2. Remove the paper from the webbing, then fuse the fleece to the wrong side of the fabric selected for the place mat back. Rough-cut this fabric slightly larger than the fleece.

3. Rough-cut the place mat front unless the fabric has a design that needs positioning or the place mat front will be decorated in a way that requires more precise cutting. If you are fusing appliqués to the front that go to the edge, do that before stitching so that the appliqué extends into the seam allowance.

4. Place the front and back with right sides together. With the fleece faceup, stitch through all layers just outside the fleece; do not catch the fleece in the seam. Leave an opening for turning.

5. Clip curves; turn and press. Stitch opening closed by hand.

6. Topstitch all around, ½ inch from the edge, or follow any other quilting lines desired.

Approximate size:
14 × 18 inches

MATERIALS NEEDED:
Paper-backed fusible webbing
Polyester fleece or low-loft quilt batting
Appropriate threads for top-stitching
Fabric for front and back of each place mat

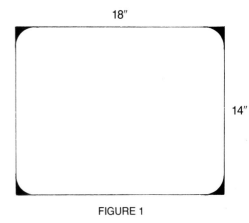

FIGURE 1

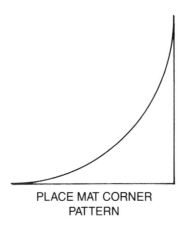

PLACE MAT CORNER
PATTERN

Serged Napkins

Approximate size:
18 inches square

MATERIALS NEEDED:
Two 18-inch squares of fabric
  for each napkin
Decorative thread
Fabric glue stick

Many serged napkins are made from one layer of fabric that is slightly heavier than a cotton print. Using two layers of printed cotton will hide the wrong or less attractive side of both layers. As a bonus, these beautiful napkins have a rich feel that comes from the weight of two layers of fabric. If you use a different fabric for each side, the napkins are even more unique and versatile.

A note about decorative thread—while you can use regular sewing thread, there are decorative threads available that add an extra touch of sophistication to these already elegant napkins. Consider using a metallic thread such as Sulky™ or other high-luster rayon thread, a wooly nylon thread which gives a full, soft edge, or one of the variegated threads now available. A decorative thread is generally threaded through the upper looper, but follow the instructions in your serger manual for complete directions.

1. Preshrink your fabric. Because napkins will be washed regularly, this is a must!

2. For each napkin, cut two pieces of fabric to the desired size.

3. Touch the glue stick to a few places on the wrong side of one fabric piece. This is how the two layers are "basted" together. (If you use pins instead, keep them toward the napkin center for your serger's sake.)

4. Place the two layers with wrong sides together. Smooth out any wrinkles or bumps.

5. Using a rolled hem setting or attachment and following your manual instructions, serge the raw edges of each napkin. Trim threads; press.

Ruffled Napkins

Approximate size:
18 inches square

MATERIALS NEEDED:
Two 16½-inch squares of fabric
  for each napkin
65 inches of a 1-inch-wide
  (finished) ruffle, made or
  purchased (use two 2¾ × 45-
  inch strips to make a fabric
  ruffle)

This is a wonderful way to use *coordinating* fabric scraps—use different fabrics for each side of the napkin, another for the ruffle, and a fourth for the napkin ring.

If you are making a ruffle, cut two 2¾ × 45-inch strips. Sew the two pieces together at the short ends, forming a continuous circle. Fold the fabric in half lengthwise and use a pin to mark off each quarter of the length (Figure 1). Use your favorite method and up to ⅜-inch seam allowance to gather the raw edges. Gather evenly until the circle is approximately 65 inches in diameter.

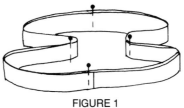

FIGURE 1

1. Pin or baste the ruffle onto the right side of one napkin piece. Match the ruffle's quarter marks with the middle of each side of the napkin square (Figure 2).

2. Stitch the front and back squares together with the ruffle between the layers; leave a small opening in one side for turning.

3. Turn inside out and press. Sew the opening closed by hand.

4. Topstitch ⅜ inch from the edge for a flat edge.

Gathered Napkin Rings

Creating something as small as a napkin ring from holiday print fabrics will add a festive touch to any table setting.

1. Fold each fabric scrap in half lengthwise. Seam the long sides together to create a tube.

2. Turn the tube inside out and press, centering the seam on the back or wrong side of the napkin ring (Figure 1).

3. Topstitch ⅝ inch from each long edge of the tube and down the center (Figure 2).

4. Cut two 5-inch lengths of elastic; thread them through the two center channels to gather the fabric.

5. When the elastic is all the way through the channel, stitch the raw ends together.

6. For a neat finish on the closing seam, zigzag or serge the seam allowance.

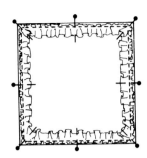

FIGURE 2

Approximate size:
2¾ inches tall

MATERIALS NEEDED (for each napkin ring):
10 inches of ½-inch-wide elastic
One 6 × 12-inch fabric scrap

FIGURE 1

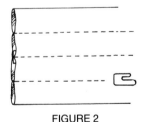

FIGURE 2

My Favorite Apron

Throughout this book, several holiday appliqué designs are included for this apron. However, if you don't have the time or inclination for appliqué, just make the apron using a wonderful holiday print.

This is my favorite apron because the unique one-piece strap tunnels through the facings and becomes both the neck and waistline ties, making it super adjustable.

Approximate size:
Fits an average adult
man or woman

MATERIALS NEEDED:
⅞ yard of fabric for small apron and strap
1 yard of fabric for large apron and strap

Note: If a contrasting strap is desired, you will need ¼ yard for the small apron or ⅓ yard for the large apron

27

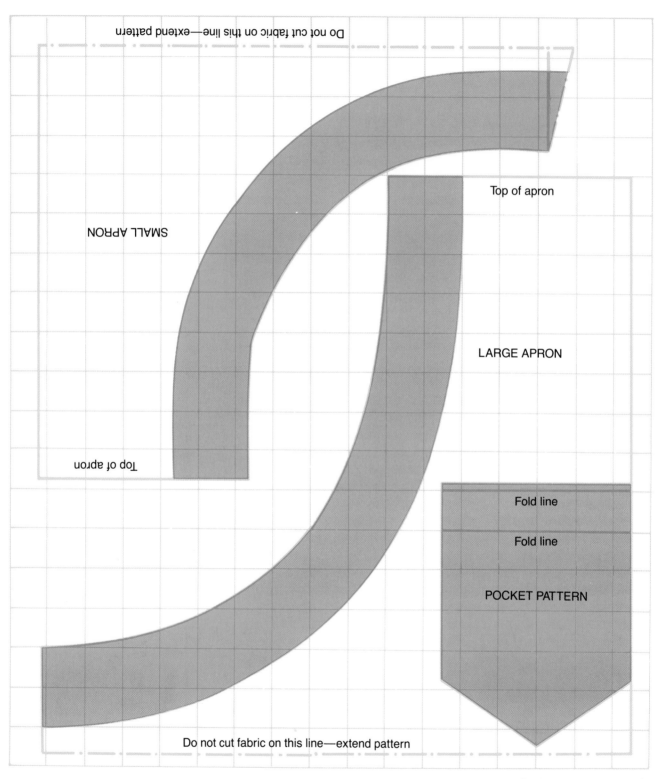

Do not cut fabric on this line—extend pattern

SMALL APRON

Top of apron

LARGE APRON

Top of apron

Fold line

Fold line

POCKET PATTERN

Do not cut fabric on this line—extend pattern

MY FAVORITE APRON PATTERNS

Scale: 1 square = 1 inch

Cutting the Apron

1. Enlarge the apron patterns from the grid on page 28. Lengthen the paper pattern now, or mark the length on the fabric as directed in Step 4.

2. The apron cutting layout, right, is not to scale. As the two sizes of aprons and the optional appliqué designs will fit the fabric differently, this diagram shows a general layout. The important point is that the lengthwise fold in the fabric is off-center, leaving a single layer of material extending for the belt, or for your scrap bag if you want a contrasting belt.

3. Pin the top of the bib pattern at one end of the fold. If you are making the apron for a person who is particularly large or small, move the pattern to one side of the center front fold to allow for more or less girth in the body of the apron.

4. Determine the desired finished length of the apron. Average length for the small apron is 28 inches, 33 inches for large. Add 1½ inches for a hem. To extend the center line to the desired length, measure down the fold to the correct length and mark. For the bottom, draw a line perpendicular to the fold. At the side, continue the underarm line straight down until it intersects the bottom line.

5. Position the facing pattern as shown on the cutting layout.

6. Mark three 2½-inch-wide strips lengthwise on the single layer of fabric as shown in the cutting layout. These should total about 90 inches for the smaller apron and 108 inches for the large.

7. Cut when all marking is complete.

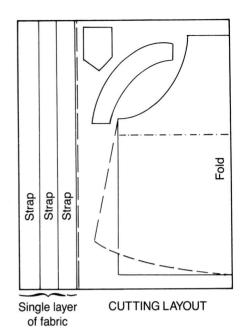

Strap
Strap
Strap

Fold

Single layer of fabric

CUTTING LAYOUT

Two More Feminine Versions

To give the apron a more feminine style, angle the side seam, round the bottom, make double-ended darts, and add a 3- to 4-inch ruffle at the bottom. (Don't forget to clip the darts at the center.) This variation is shown on the cutting layout above.

To make the original small apron more formfitting, simply add the darts as described above.

Sewing the Apron

1. With right sides together, pin and sew facings to the apron along the curved underarm. Stitch, using a ½-inch-wide seam allowance. Clip the seam to allow it to spread. Press the seam allowance toward the facing and topstitch through the seam allowance and facing only.

2. While facings are opened out, press under ¼ inch and then another 1 inch across the top edge of the apron and hem, stitching over the opened-out facings (Figure 1). Press and hem the bottom edge in the same manner. At the sides, press under ¼ inch, then another ¼ inch and hem, again stitching over the opened-out facings as illustrated.

3. Press raw edges of facings under ¼ inch; stitch, if necessary. Press the facings flat against the wrong side of the apron. Stitch facings to apron along the hemmed edge of the facing only. Leave the facings open at each end to make a tunnel for the strap.

4. Add an appropriate appliqué if desired. Make darts, if desired, but be aware that darts and an appliqué can get mixed up. Plan carefully.

5. To make the straps, sew the strap pieces together to make one long piece (90 inches long for small apron and 108 inches for large apron). Press both long raw edges in to meet in the center (Figure 2). Press the strip in half lengthwise again as shown, then topstitch along both edges through all four thicknesses of fabric.

6. Run the strap through the facing tunnel on one side (Figure 3); allow a loop for the neck, then run it through the other facing. Pull the strap through so that it will tie at the center back.

7. If adding a pocket, make a narrow hem at the top edge. Fold 1 inch down, right sides together, and stitch ¼ inch from the edge on both sides (Figure 4). Clip the corner; turn and press. Press the remaining raw edges under ¼ inch. Position pocket as desired; topstitch in place. Reinforce topstitching at corners.

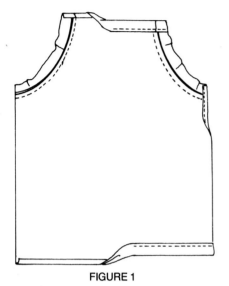

FIGURE 1

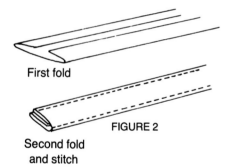

First fold

FIGURE 2

Second fold
and stitch

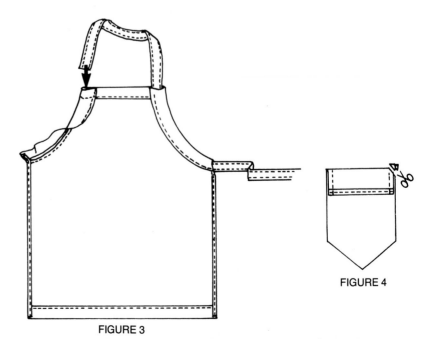

FIGURE 4

FIGURE 3

WREATHS

Wreaths are another generic item that can be fabricated and trimmed for almost any holiday season. Basic instructions are included for four styles—Puff, Shag, Poked, and Tied.

The Puff Wreath

Puff wreaths are made by creating individual stuffed rectangular "pillows," sewing them together into a unit that resembles a life jacket, then wrapping and securing that unit around a cardboard base or wreath form. The wreath shown below is made from a collection of Halloween prints. Four of its rectangles have some piecing, three of them with extensive string piecing (see page 22).

    1. Using the corner pattern, below, cut corners off each scrap rectangle.

    2. Fold and press tucks in all four corners of each rectangle by creasing on line A and folding to line B as shown in Figure 1. The fold of each tuck should go toward the short end of the rectangle.

Approximate size:
18 inches in diameter

MATERIALS NEEDED:
Twelve 6½ × 12½-inch fabric scraps
½ yard of muslin for backing
18-inch square of cardboard or foam-core board to make a ring or a purchased 16-inch-diameter wreath form
Art knife to cut ring

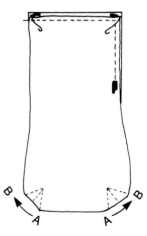

FIGURE 1

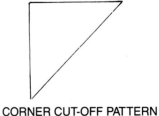

CORNER CUT-OFF PATTERN
PUFFY WREATH

31

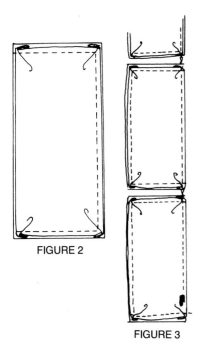

FIGURE 2

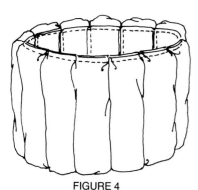

FIGURE 3

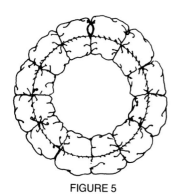

FIGURE 4

3. Cut twelve 4¾ × 11-inch rectangles of muslin.

4. Pin a muslin rectangle to the wrong side of each tucked print rectangle, aligning the edges of both pieces (Figure 1). If the corners don't match perfectly, that's okay.

5. Using a ¼-inch seam allowance, start stitching at the first corner. Pivot ¼ inch from corners 2 and 3. Don't worry about small puckers at the corners; this area will not be visible. If you fold the corners as suggested, you can sew around three sides and catch all four corners (Figure 2). Leave the fourth side open for stuffing. It is easiest to complete this step on all the pillows, then stuff all of them. At this point, the raw edges are still exposed; they will be covered when they are sewn into the next seam.

6. Stuff the pillows lightly so they will bend nicely around the frame. Polyester fiberfill gives the nicest hand and is washable. Brands vary, but 4 to 6 ounces should easily fill one wreath.

7. Sew up the fourth side. You can do this easily and quickly by making a long chain of pillows, never lifting your sewing machine presser foot (Figure 3). Then clip the pillows apart.

8. Arrange the pillows in the desired order. With the right sides of the print fabrics touching, sew the long side seams together. A zipper foot may be helpful. Make a complete circle (Figure 4).

9. To make a ring from foam-core or cardboard, cut a 16-inch-diameter circle. Cut an 11½-inch-diameter circle out of the center. The resulting ring is 2¼ inches wide. Foam-core, available at art supply stores, is sturdy enough to cut just this one piece, but it must be cut with an art knife. If you are using corrugated cardboard, cut two more cardboard rings, each slightly smaller. Stack and glue the three rings together so the edges of the ring become slightly rounded.

10. Put the pillow unit inside the wreath ring with the muslin side against the ring. Bring the pillows around the ring and pin the edges together on the back, matching the rectangles.

11. Before sewing the back shut by hand, cut a 1 × 15-inch strip from the remaining muslin; run this strip under the patchwork, around the frame, and knot it. Tie a second knot to make a loop outside the wreath for hanging (Figure 5).

12. Add ribbon bows, charms, or other adornments suitable for the holiday. The Halloween wreath shown has assorted ribbons tied between the puffs. Pull the ribbons tight to accent the puff.

FIGURE 5

Three Free-Spirited Wreaths

The Shag Wreath, Poked Wreath, and Tied Wreath share several things in common.

1. They really are scrappy. It isn't necessary to have exact amounts of anything.

2. The fabric pieces all have exposed cut edges. Pinking shears create edges with visual interest, but there is lots of cutting, so using a rotary cutter to cut bias strips or squares is a less painful way to eliminate fraying.

3. Both sides of the material are visible, which puts a special emphasis on using solid fabrics or overdyed prints.

4. Lots of different materials—such as velvet ribbons, metallic trims, and nylon net—blend beautifully with more conventional fabric scraps and add perky touches to the wreath.

5. Because they are dependent on perky loose ends for their good looks, shipping and storage are both very demanding to avoid squashing them.

6. They each do best on a different type of wreath form. The finished size is dependent on the wreath form selected.

The Shag Wreath is the only one of the three that requires any sewing. It is best made on a firm plastic-foam form. Cover the wreath by spiral-wrapping 2 × 45-inch bias strips around the form. Secure all loose ends.

To make the shag covering, cut bias strips of assorted fabrics ½ inch to 1 inch wide and 4 inches to 5½ inches long. Short strips are perkier than long strips. Experiment to achieve your favorite look.

Machine-stitch across the squeezed center of one strip. Do not stop, lift the presser foot, or cut the thread, but just squeeze a second strip and stitch it. Keep going while you create what appears to be a giant kite tail.

To apply the shag, zigzag a bead of hot glue for several inches on the top surface and slightly down the sides of the fabric-wrapped wreath. Then zigzag the shag string atop the glue, keeping the loose ends of the fabrics up and away from the glue.

Decorate the wreath with bows, ribbons, metallic-wire novelties, and other embellishments. Make a hanging loop.

The Poked Wreath must be made on a porous foam wreath that you can poke with a skewer or a small, dull pencil, and that's all you do.

Cut 4-inch squares (on the diagonal or with pinking shears) of as few as four coordinating fabrics or as many fabrics as desired. With your skewer or pencil positioned in the center of each fabric square, poke the fabric into the wreath form less than ½ inch. No glue is necessary.

It is easiest if you work in four rows, but make them only semi-orderly. Poking in an orderly row in either direction can weaken the wreath form. Add bows or other appropriate decorations.

The Tied Wreath is probably the easiest, but the least spontaneous, of these three wreaths. It works best on a wire form, but can also be made on a small foam form.

For wire shapes, cut 1 × 6-inch bias strips. Fold each strip in half and place it under the wire frame. Bring the loop created by the fold in the center over the top of the wire and put the two cut ends through the loop. Pull snugly to tighten the loop onto the wire. If you are working with print fabrics, pay careful attention to the way the fabric twists to maximize the right side of the fabric.

Continue around the ring. All fabric strips can match or two can alternate or a large variety of scraps can be looped randomly. Add appropriate decorative trims.

CHAPTER FOUR

A. BEAR FOR ALL SEASONS

A. Bear appears in every holiday chapter of this book. That may seem generous, but it was done to show that the same pattern can be fabricated for different holidays.

If you want to make one A. Bear with multiple accessories, that is exactly what we did with the white wool bear originally made to celebrate St. Patrick's Day. On page 95, you'll find him decked out in a variety of this book's holiday outfits.

The Basic Bear

Materials

A. Bear was designed to be made from fabrics other than fur, but he can be furry if you like. Patterns for fur bears are usually too skinny when made from wool or cotton or taffeta, but not A. Bear! Even though he was designed for flat, woven fabrics, a low-pile fabric also works well.

When cutting and sewing pile fabric, remember these rules. Position all patterns with the nap going in the same direction so all of A. Bear's fur "grows" the same way. Be careful as you pin to tuck the pile in and down toward the seam. Machine-sew 8–10 stitches per inch so you can pull some of the pile caught in the seam allowance to the outside of A. Bear. This helps lessen the look of a part that results from a regular seam in pile fabric.

Most of the bears shown were made with purchased bear eyes and nose sets. These have ½-inch long rods extending from the center back of each piece, and are secured with disks. These sets come in several sizes; A. Bear's eyes are approximately ⅝ inch in diameter.

Lining

Most of my bears are lined with Thermore™—a soft, thin, washable quilt batting that does not beard. It adds firmness to cotton fabrics and makes stuffing technique less critical by putting an additional soft layer between A. Bear's outside and the wads of stuffing. Fleece will also work, but it is a little thicker and more dense. Some of the heavier fabrics used were not lined at all. If you are using a heavy wool or a low pile, then you do not need to line A. Bear.

If you choose to line your bear, cut a lining piece for each body piece; the ears have only one layer of lining. Lay matching pieces of fabric and lining together. As you assemble the bear, treat each set as one piece of fabric.

Cutting

Trace the A. Bear patterns on pages 38–43; be sure to mark grain lines on each paper pattern. From the bear fabric, cut four ears, four arms, and one front; cut two each of all the other pieces.

Approximate size:
25 inches tall

MATERIALS NEEDED:
⅝ yard of 60-inch-wide fabric or ⅞ yard of 45-inch-wide fabric
⅞ yard of fleece or Thermore™ (optional, see below)
Two ⅞- or 1-inch-diameter buttons for arms
Polyester stuffing
Purchased eyes and nose (optional, see below)

Making the Head

Unless otherwise indicated, all seams are sewn with fabric right sides together and with ¼-inch seam allowance. Trim seams if necessary, and clip curves. Press seams open after each step.

1. Stay-stitch the neck line on all four head pieces.

2. Stitch front head pieces together at center front. Stitch back head pieces together at center back.

3. To make each ear, stitch curved edge of two ear pieces together; clip seam allowances and turn ear right side out.

4. Stitch a gathering line across the bottom of each ear, but concentrate the gathers closer together in the area between the dots.

5. Baste ears to right side of front head piece, between markings indicated on front head pattern (Figure 1).

6. Complete the head by stitching back to front, leaving open at the base. Clip seam allowances, then turn head right side out.

7. Position the eyes, making a tiny hole in the fabric just large enough to push the eye rod through; secure it on the back side of the fabric with the disk (Figure 2). The nose can be secured through the seam. Cut a stitch or two, if necessary. Stacked buttons, such as a smaller blue button on top of a pearl button, can be substituted for decorative bears' eyes (Figure 3). If you are making A. Bear for a child, you may prefer to substitute embroidered eyes and nose for safety (Figure 4). None of the bears in this book have a mouth, but one can be added with an outline stitch.

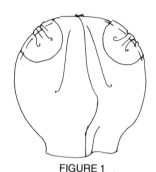

FIGURE 1

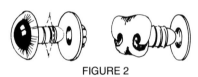

FIGURE 2

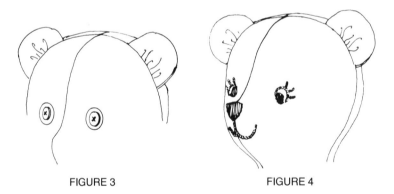

FIGURE 3   FIGURE 4

Making the Legs

1. For each leg, fold right sides together along fold line. Stitch the back leg seam, beginning at the dot at the center back marked on the leg pattern and tapering the stitching to a full ¼-inch seam allowance as shown. Stitch around the foot and up to the top of the leg. Leave the top open. Clip seam allowances and turn legs right side out.

2. Stuff the foot firmly, but stuff very lightly above the knee area. Heavily stuffed upper legs will push the bear backwards and keep it from sitting up.

3. Stitch top opening shut with a ⅛-inch seam allowance.

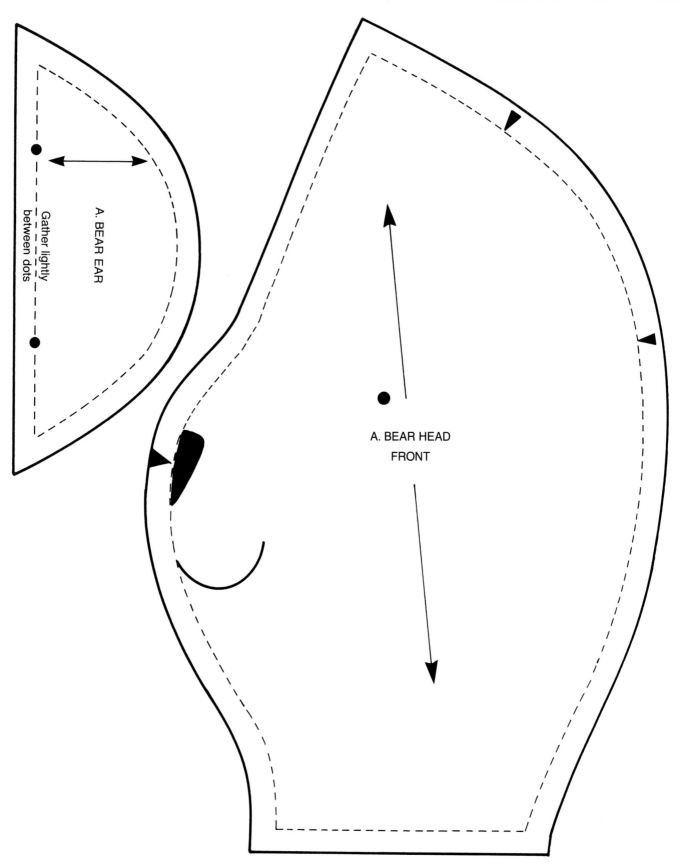

A. BEAR EAR

Gather lightly
between dots

A. BEAR HEAD
FRONT

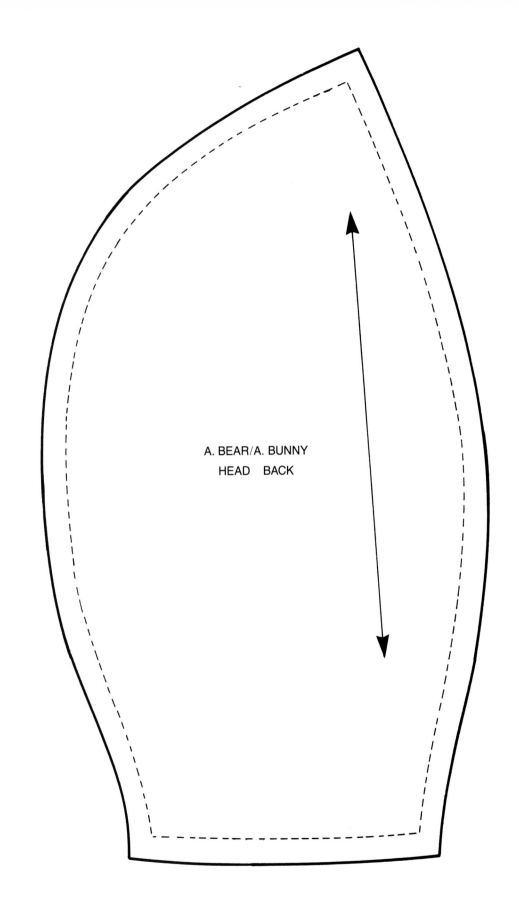

A. BEAR/A. BUNNY
HEAD   BACK

A. BEAR/A. BUNNY BODY

FRONT

Center front • Place on fold

Add bear legs to this side

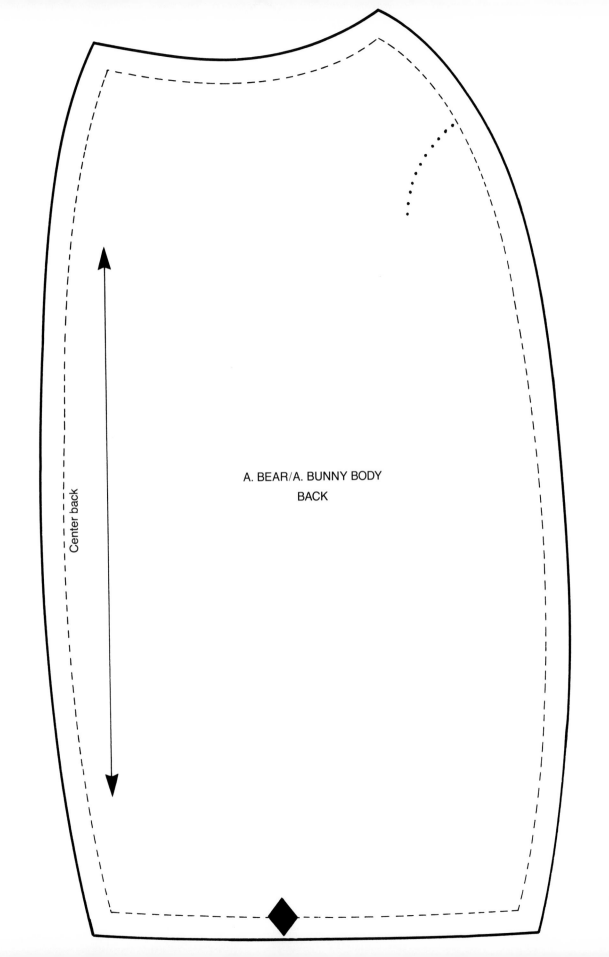

A. BEAR/A. BUNNY BODY
BACK

Center back

41

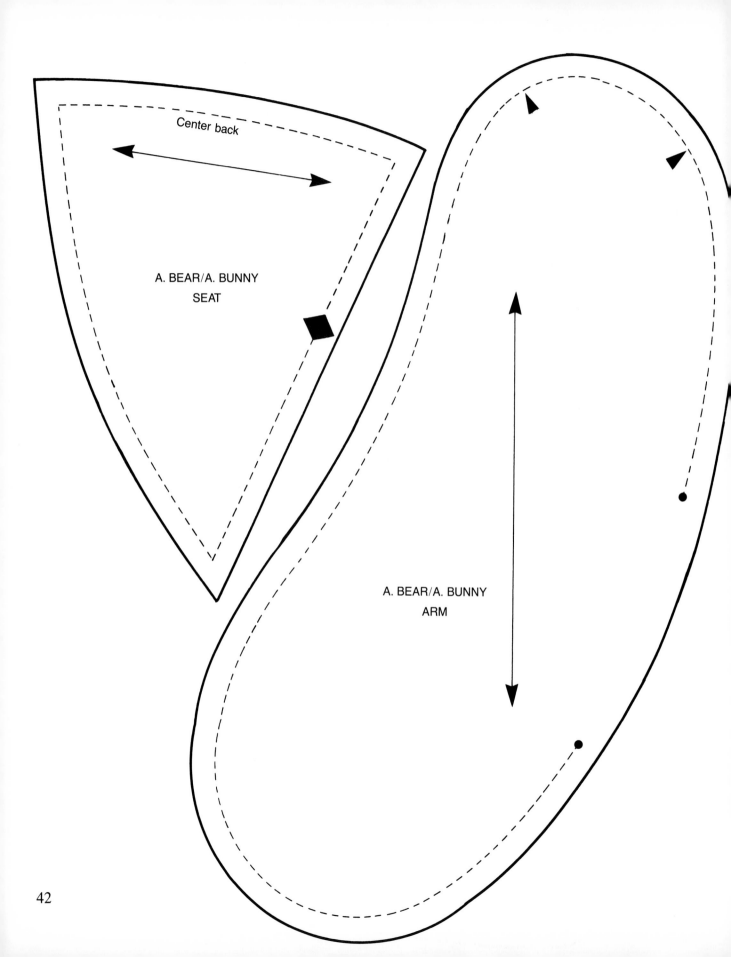

Center back

A. BEAR/A. BUNNY
SEAT

A. BEAR/A. BUNNY
ARM

42

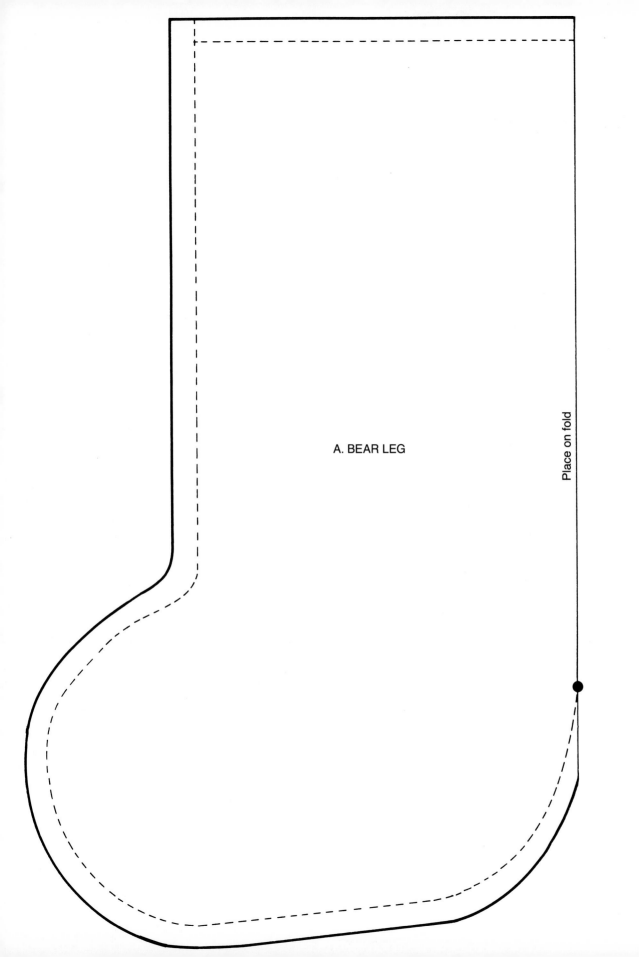

A. BEAR LEG

Place on fold

43

Assembling the Body

1. Stay-stitch neck lines on all three body pieces.

2. Baste stuffed legs to front body piece (Figure 5). At this point, the toes should touch the front body piece or they won't point forward when the bear is completed.

3. Stitch back body pieces together at center back, leaving 4 to 5 inches open in center back for turning later.

4. Stitch seat sections together at center back.

5. Ease seat and attach to body back, matching back seams and notches (Figure 6).

6. Make a "leg sandwich" by enclosing the legs when pinning front and back body sections together. Stitch front and back together at side seams first. Ease and stitch seat section to bottom of body front (Figure 7).

7. Leaving A. Bear wrong side out, place head inside top of body with right sides together and matching raw edges. Match back and side seams; A. Bear's nose should be pressed into his belly.

8. Sew head to body from inside, easing slightly if necessary (Figure 8).

9. Turn entire bear through back opening, starting with one leg, then the other, and finally the rest of the body and the head.

10. Stuff body and head firmly through the back opening. For a purely decorative A. Bear, added weight in his bottom provides better balance for sitting. (Aquarium gravel works well in a plastic bag filled so it can shift and adapt to whatever surface the bear is sitting on.)

11. Slip-stitch center back opening.

12. Stitch arm pieces together, leaving open between dots for turning. Clip, turn, and loosely stuff arms, so they are plump but not firm. Slip-stitch opening shut.

13. Either stitch a decorative button at the shoulder end of the arm, or mark which end will be attached to the body. Position buttons with equal amounts of space on each side (Figure 9). Slip-stitch arms to body between arrows shown on arm pattern.

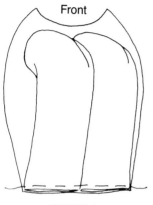

Front

FIGURE 5

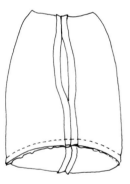

FIGURE 6

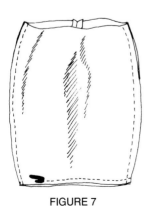

FIGURE 7

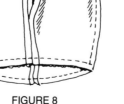

FIGURE 8

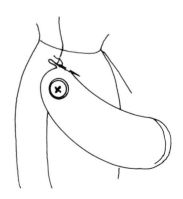

FIGURE 9

CHAPTER FIVE

MERRY CHRISTMAS

A. Bear's Christmas Hat and Vest

Making the Hat

1. Cut an 11 × 19-inch piece of print fabric for the hat and a 6 × 19-inch strip of coordinating fabric for the hat band.

2. Press ¼-inch seam allowance to the wrong side along one long edge of the hat band. With right sides together, sew the other edge of the band to one long edge of the hat.

3. Seam the short ends of this piece together, making a tube (Figure 1).

4. Fold the band up inside the hat, with right side of band showing, bringing the pressed seam allowance just above the stitching line.

5. To secure the band, stitch in the ditch from the outside of the hat or stitch it in place by hand.

6. Create the taper in the hat by making four darts. Find the quarter points (fold in half and fold in half again), and make darts 1½ inches deep and 6½ inches long. Cut away excess (Figure 2).

7. Turn back a seam allowance at the top edge; gather top of hat into a point and secure gathering thread. Turn hat right side out and add a decorative pom-pom on top.

Approximate size:
Sized to fit bear

MATERIALS NEEDED:
½ yard of Christmas print fabric for hat and vest
½ yard of coordinating fabric for hat band and vest lining
Three ⅜-inch-diameter gold buttons
16 inches of 3-inch-wide wire-edged pleated ribbon for bow tie
Large pom-pom for hat

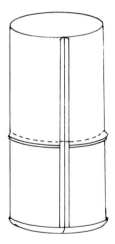

FIGURE 1

FIGURE 2

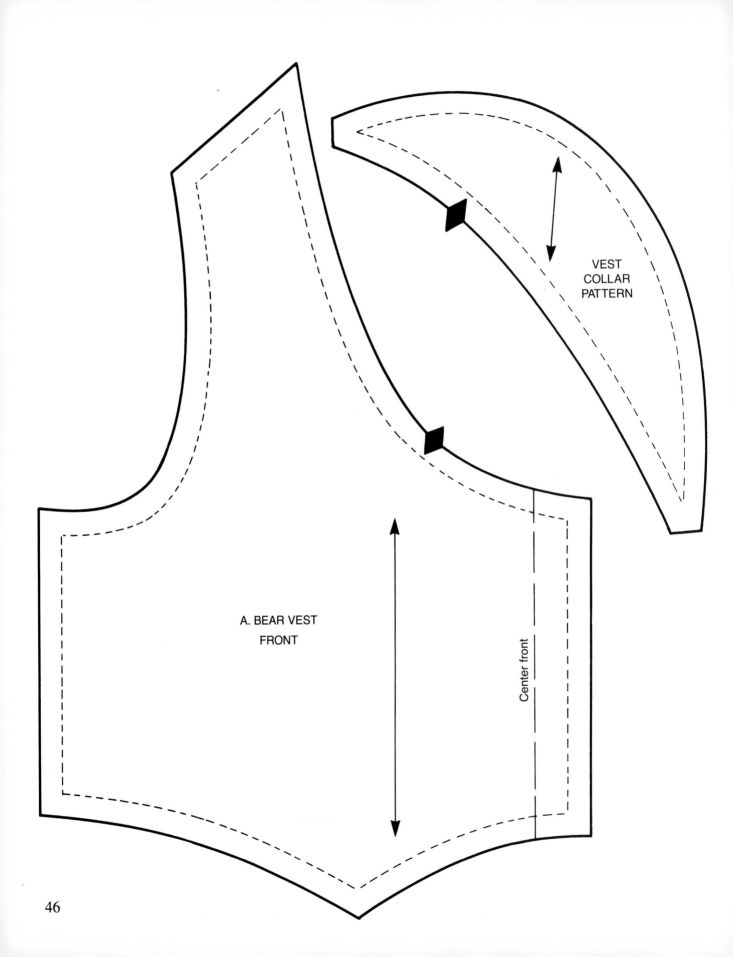

VEST
COLLAR
PATTERN

A. BEAR VEST
FRONT

Center front

46

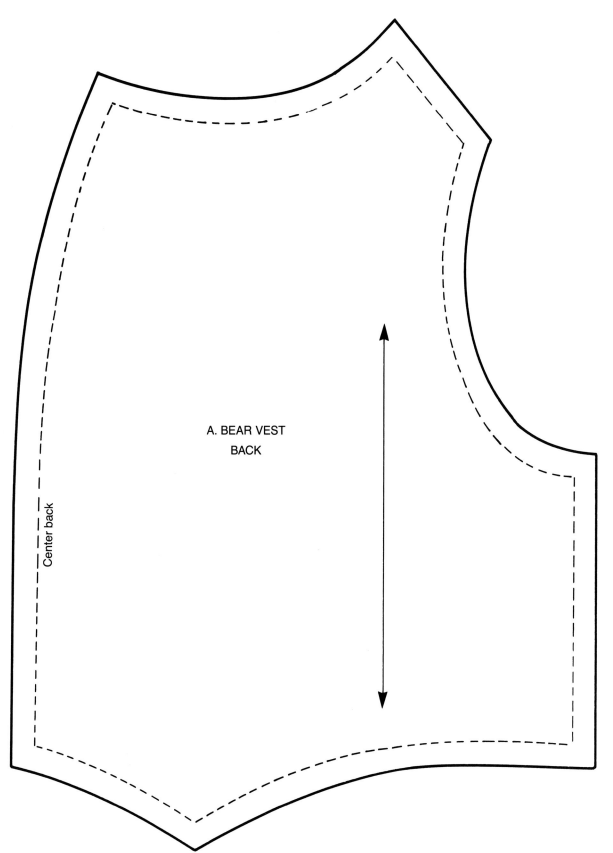

A. BEAR VEST
BACK

Center back

Making the Vest

1. Trace the vest patterns on pages 46 and 47. Cut two fronts and two backs from both the lining fabric and the Christmas print. Cut four collar pieces from the coordinating fabric.

2. Stitch two pairs of collar pieces together, leaving the notched edge open. Clip, turn, and press.

3. Lay right and left collar sections in position on vest fronts, right side up, with the wider end of each collar section touching the center front dot. Match notches. Baste in place (Figure 1).

4. Stitch center back seam of vest.

5. Stitch vest fronts to back at shoulder seams only.

6. On each lining piece, press back the side seam allowances where left, right, and back pieces will be attached. Stitch center back and shoulder seams in the same manner as for the vest.

7. With right sides of vest and lining together and seams matching, stitch vest and lining together as shown in Figure 2.

8. Trim and clip seams. Turn vest right side out through one open side seam. Slip-stitch both side seams (Figure 3).

9. Add small gold buttons to vest. Make button holes, or use snaps or Velcro™ for the closure.

Adding the Bow Tie

Tie wired, pleated gold ribbon in a bow around A. Bear's neck. Adjust bow and trim the ribbon ends as desired.

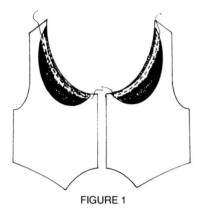

FIGURE 1

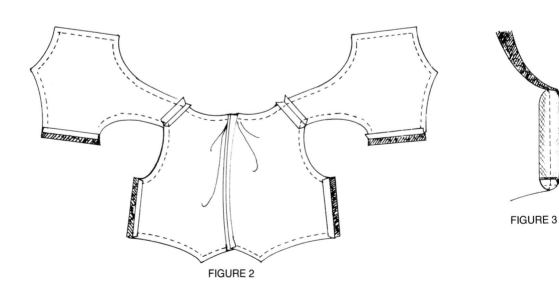

FIGURE 2

FIGURE 3

Winter Walk
(Old St. Nick Wall Hanging)

A starry night, a moonlit forest, and Old St. Nick are combined in a wall hanging that is the perfect decorative highlight for an old-fashioned or antique Christmas theme. This is the kind of project best undertaken when you have time to enjoy rummaging through your scraps for just the right fabric and standing back to check the effect of each addition. The effort will be worth it as you enjoy St. Nick year after year. If you have a design wall (see Chapter 2, page 12), this is the time to use it.

For this project, positioning fabrics randomly is almost as important as the assortment of fabrics. Study the picture on page 54 to get a feeling for the number and use of the prints. Remember, as always, your wall hanging will be uniquely yours because your fabrics are different. Don't go crazy trying to duplicate these fabrics.

Making the Stars

Yes, there are six different stars. They were designed that way to give the feeling of distance. Trace the star patterns on page 52; the letter designations on these patterns correspond to the stars identified on the Assembly Diagram, left.

1. Select fabrics. If you aren't used to working with lots of different fabrics, this is a good time to try things you wouldn't normally put together, such as navy blue and black, or cotton prints and gold lamé. To help you decide fabric position, put a large piece of navy fabric on your design wall. Rough-cut squares and triangles to represent star points and centers; pin them in place, moving them until you are satisfied. Add rough-cut sky sections to give it more interest. Add and subtract fabrics without panic. Wait until you have finished this planning process to worry about cutting accurate pieces unless you have a very limited amount of a certain fabric.

2. Cut star and sky pieces. If you have even a slight inclination to make the Star Pillows, cut twice as many pieces now so you won't have to locate all the fabrics a second time. Pay attention when cutting the star points because all of the points except the smallest are asymmetrical and must be cut in the right direction to go together properly. The easiest way to keep track is to cut with the fabric faceup, laying the pattern in the same orientation as desired for the finished piece. As you cut, lay or pin the pieces in place on a firm, portable surface such as a piece of corrugated or foam-core board.

3. Piece each of the six stars. Think of them as nine-patch patchwork. Assemble the stars by first piecing the points into units, then join these units with squares to complete the block (Figure 1).

4. Referring to the assembly diagram, join the stars and extra sky pieces to make the top half of the wall hanging. Because there may be considerable difference in the finished sizes of these units, cut the sky pieces larger or smaller to make this section the correct size. Check the diagram as you go.

Approximate size:
32 × 42 inches

MATERIALS NEEDED:
Scraps of navy, slate blue, yellow, cream, green, brown, and dark red fabrics
Scraps of gold lamé (optional)
15 × 18 inches of low-pile imitation fur
Hair and beard material such as goat hair or crepe wool
10 × 20 inches *each* of fleece and fusible webbing
1 yard *each* of backing fabric and quilt batting
⅜ yard of purchased drapery cord for belt

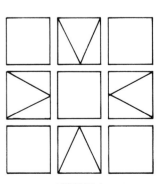

FIGURE 1

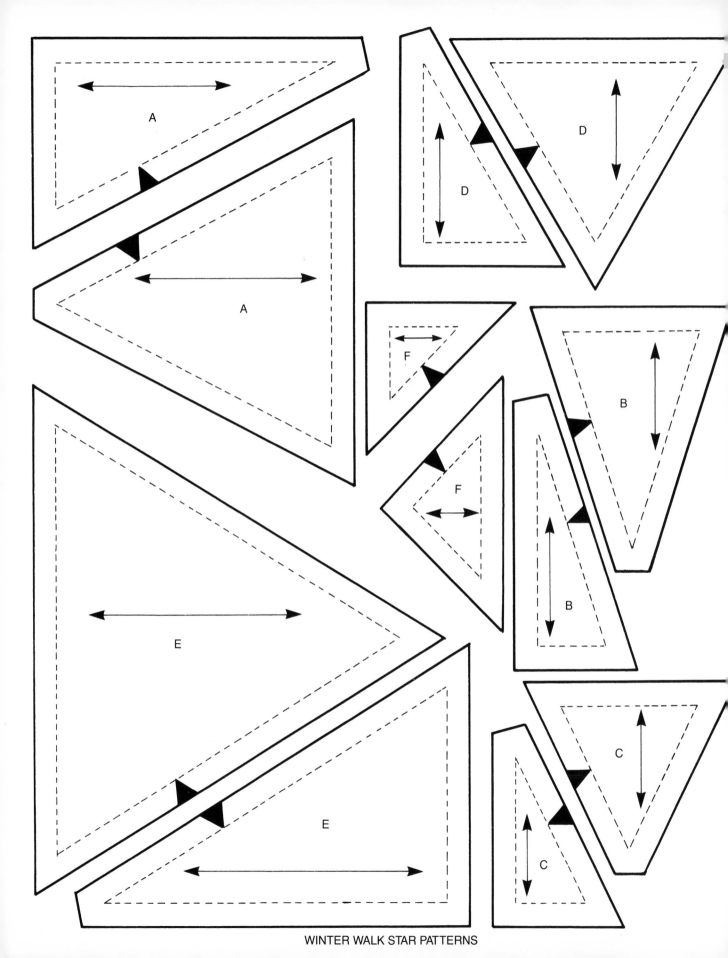

WINTER WALK STAR PATTERNS

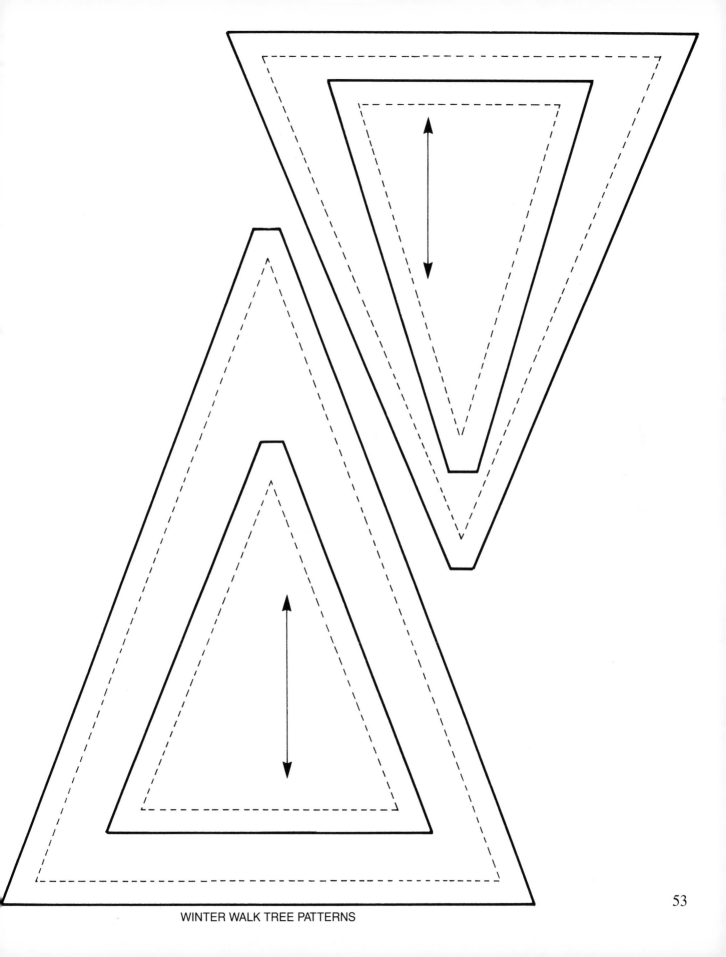

WINTER WALK TREE PATTERNS

53

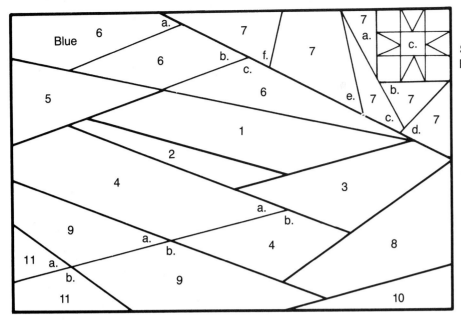

STITCH AND FLIP GUIDE
FOR WINTER WALK WALL HANGING

For example, the finished B star should be half as wide as star E. The dotted lines around the small F star next to the B star represent seams of sky fabrics added to make a square as big as the B star.

Making the Lower Half Background

Work on a muslin background larger than the 19×27 inches of the finished bottom section. Mine was approximately 24×30 inches.

Refer to the Stitch and Flip Guide, above, and the Cutting List, right, to cut fabric pieces for this section.

The Stitch and Flip Guide is just a guide; don't take it too literally. The size of each piece in this section can be flexible except the position of the C star, so it is a good idea to prepare Unit 7 first and keep it handy to help determine how the pieces are going together.

Using the stitch and flip technique described in Chapter 2, start by joining units 1 and 2 and proceed numerically, pre-piecing the units that are divided into segments. It is easy to spend too much time here. Remember the background will be covered with string-pieced trees and St. Nick. The purpose, of course, is to look like mountains so the jagged sky line and the different fabrics create an illusion of distance. When the fabrics cover the area needed, trim the background to the correct size.

Making the String-Pieced Trees

Referring to the photo, use the patterns on page 53 to cut 10 tree shapes from muslin. String-quilt tree fabric randomly atop each muslin piece.

Line and turn the trees for easy appliqué. Position the trees as desired and fuse trunks, cut by eye, in place before appliquéing the trees onto the background. Work from the back to the front to make sure the trees overlap properly. My trees were appliquéd with a machine that has an almost invisible blanket stitch.

Cutting List
Approximate fabrics needed for lower background
1. 6×20 inches
2. 3×14 inches
3. 5×13 inches
4a. 5×19 inches
4b. 5×8 inches
5. 5×11 inches
6a. 6×13 inches
6b. 6×10 inches
6c. 4×16 inches
7a. 4×6 inches
7b. 3×10 inches
7c. 4×7 inches
7d. 5-inch square
7e. 9-inch square
7f. 5×10 inches
8. 6×13 inches
9a. 4×11 inches
9b. 6×10 inches
10. 3×11 inches
11a. $2\frac{1}{2} \times 3$ inches
11b. 4×8 inches

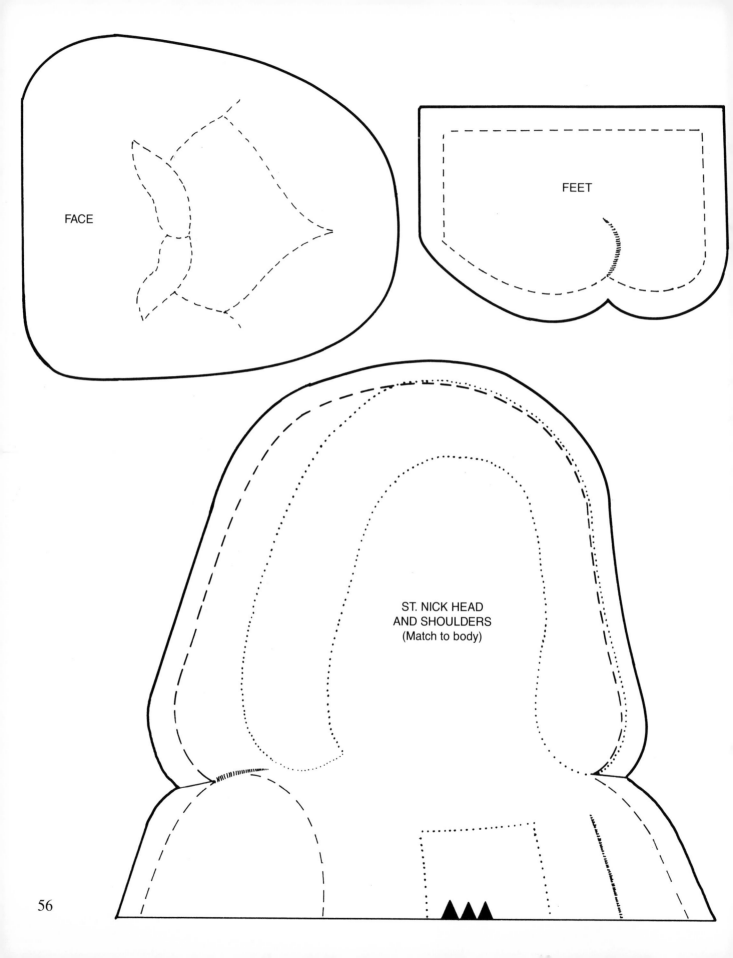

FACE

FEET

ST. NICK HEAD
AND SHOULDERS
(Match to body)

56

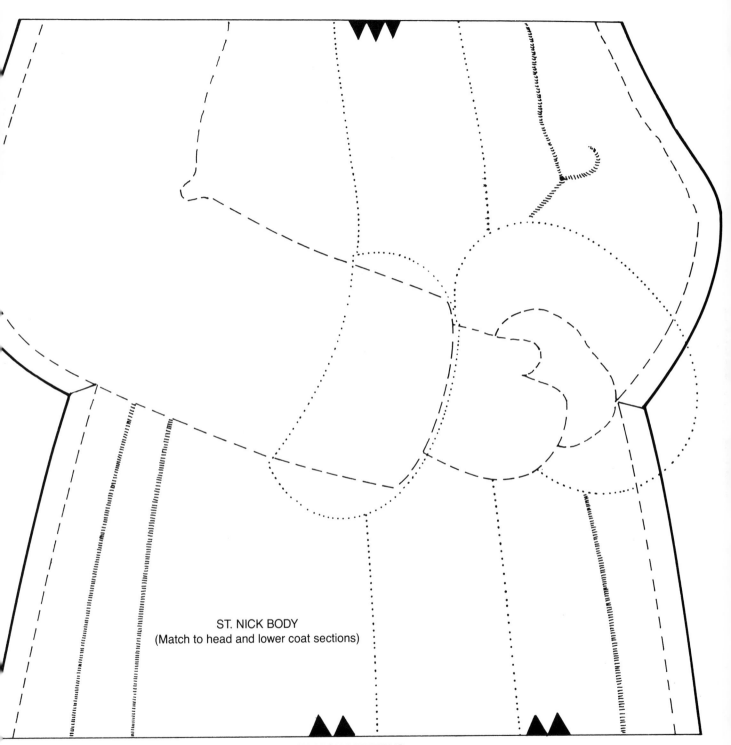

ST. NICK BODY
(Match to head and lower coat sections)

ST. NICK PATTERNS

57

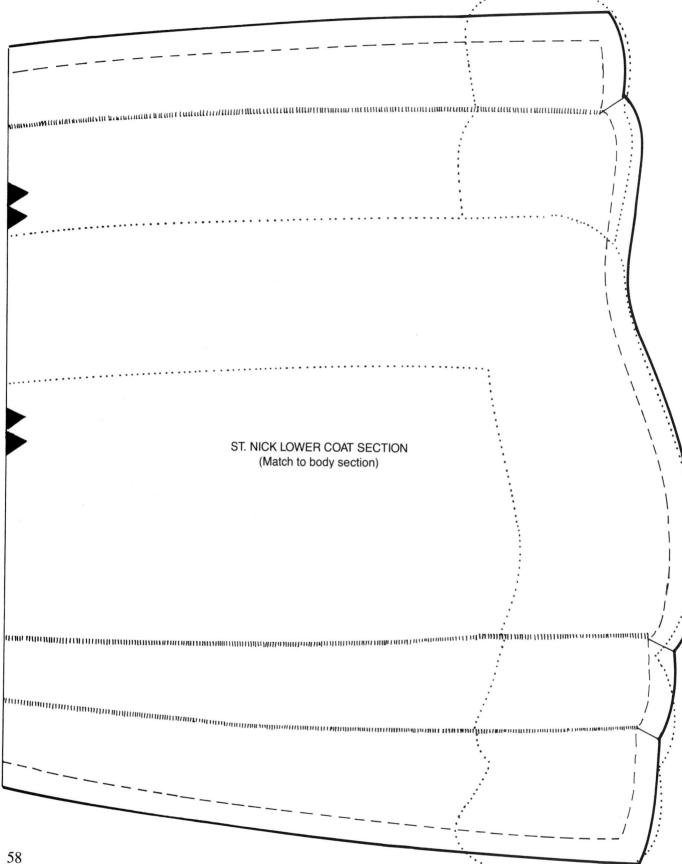

ST. NICK LOWER COAT SECTION
(Match to body section)

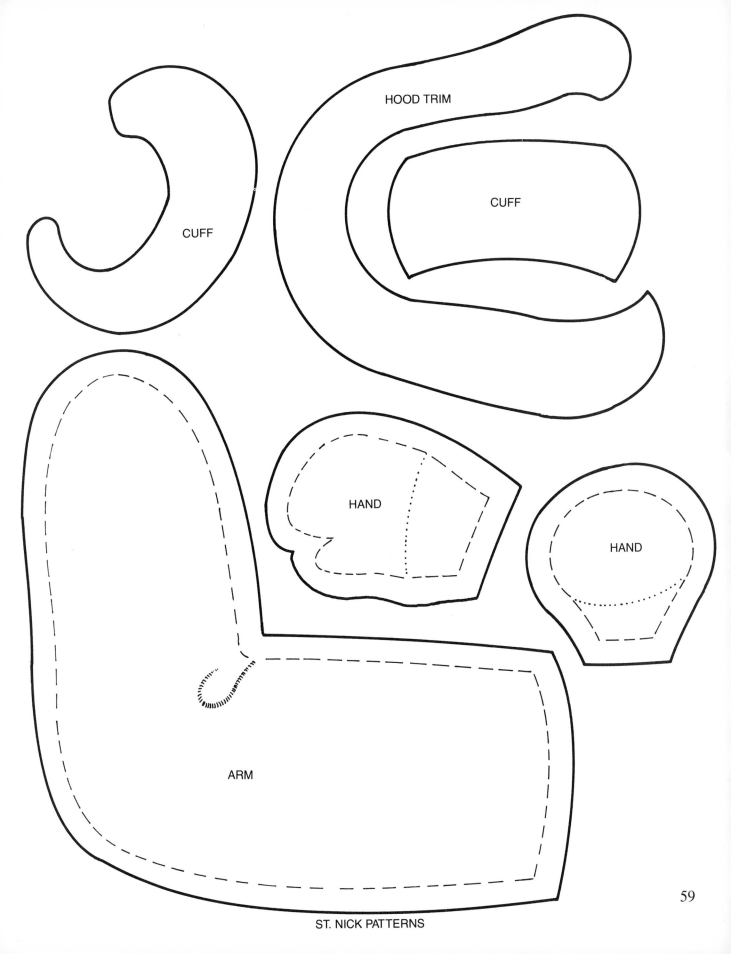

CUFF

HOOD TRIM

CUFF

HAND

HAND

ARM

59

ST. NICK PATTERNS

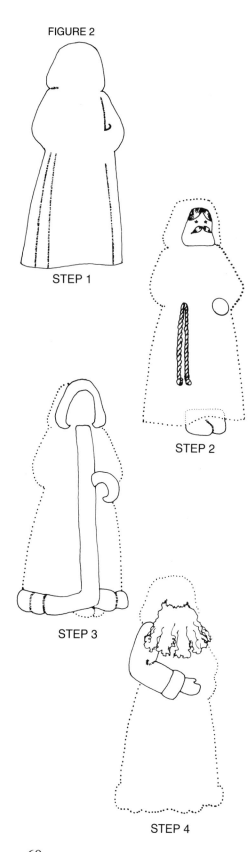

FIGURE 2

STEP 1

STEP 2

STEP 3

STEP 4

Join the upper and lower sections of the wall hanging before appliquéing the trees that overlap.

Appliqué St. Nick

The St. Nick is made as a separate unit that is appliquéd onto the finished wall hanging. You might consider an attaching technique such as Velcro™ so the dimensional unit can be removed each year for easy storage.

Make a tracing of the full-length St. Nick from the patterns on pages 56–59, connecting each pattern segment as indicated. From that pattern or the separate patterns included, trace the component sections needed.

St. Nick is made in four separate steps with dimensional arm, beard, fur, and belt (Figure 2).

1. Apply the fusible material to one side of the fleece. Using the full-length pattern, cut one body piece of fused fleece, fusible side down. Rough-cut one piece of robe fabric and one of a lining fabric slightly larger than the fleece. Fuse fleece to lining.

2. Put right side of St. Nick fabric and lining together. Stitching just outside the fleece, sew all the way around. Cut a slit where the fur trim will go and turn St. Nick through that slit or leave an opening in the seam for turning and close that opening by hand.

3. With dark thread and a narrow zigzag stitch, add the detail lines shown in Step 1 of Figure 2.

4. Appliqué the face in place, stuffing very lightly before closing completely. Sew or glue hair in place, extending it high on the forehead so the top will be covered by fur. Eyes can be embroidered or drawn.

5. Make the feet and hands using the line and turn technique described on page 20. Stitch feet and right hand in place as shown in Step 2 of Figure 2. Tack the belt cord in place as shown.

6. Cut the coat trim pieces from the fur. A razor blade or art knife is often recommended for cutting low-pile fur. Because I am not fond of those tools, I mark pattern shapes on the acrylic backing (with the pattern facedown) and carefully run my scissor points close to the knit backing. This way I can easily cut the pieces without cutting through the pile and I get the resulting clean line of a scissor cut.

7. Secure the fur pieces, except the left cuff, with a combination of glue and a little careful stitching (Step 3, Figure 2). Brush the pile over the edges to cover all traces of backing.

8. Fuse the left arm with fleece, like the St. Nick body, and stitch it in place. Add the left hand and cuff as before.

9. The beard is added last, in the same manner as for the hair (Step 4, Figure 2). The beard shown was made from real goat hair, a special gift from someone who bought it at a craft show and gave it to me, knowing that someday I would need a beard fiber. Goat hair isn't available on every corner, but there are many wonderful beard materials available.

Attach the completed St. Nick to the wall hanging when the final border is added and quilting is completed.

Finishing Details

The materials in your wall hanging will determine the width and combination of materials that will look right for a border. My Winter Walk has a ½-inch-wide border of gold lamé and a 2-inch-wide final frame of the dark red print from St. Nick's coat.

Quilt and bind the wall hanging as desired. I like to display the wall hanging accented with a beautiful bow made of wire-edged metallic ribbon.

Plain St. Nick

If the Winter Walk Wall Hanging is too big or too much of an undertaking, a simple St. Nick can be very pleasing. For the background, use a good midnight sky fabric and a snow fabric. Appliqué St. Nick in the same way as for the large wall hanging. Quilt and bind as desired.

Starry Night Pillows

If you put the Winter Walk Wall Hanging in a room where throw pillows are appropriate, the patchwork Starry Night Pillows are a pleasant way to continue the theme. Use the same patterns and follow the instructions for making the patchwork stars (page 51) to make as many different star blocks (or combinations of blocks) as you like.

Layer each pillow top with batting and backing; hand or machine quilt as desired. The pillows shown are 12–18 inches square, including ruffles.

Basic ruffle and pillow-making information follows separately, so you can make the best decision for your pillows. Specific measurements used to make ruffles for each pillow are given on page 65.

Ruffle Styles and Methods

Ruffles can be such a crucial part of a finished pillow, it is important to consider them carefully. Use the ruffle width measurements in this book as guidelines only. When you work with fabrics different from those pictured, the color, contrast, and other factors will change, so the most attractive width for each ruffle may also change. Fold each fabric to the width that you like, measure, and proceed.

Cutting. Think ahead when planning a pillow and allow a ½-inch seam allowance on the pillow's outside edge if you plan to add a ruffle. Then allow a corresponding ½-inch seam allowance on all your ruffles as well.

Cut the width of each ruffle twice as wide as the desired *finished* width *plus* two seam allowances.

Cut the length of the ruffle 2 to 2½ times the perimeter of the pillow. When multiple strips are necessary to achieve the desired length, sew them together, short end to short end. Lightweight fabrics and wider ruffles look better with extra fullness.

I cut ruffles on the straight grain, not on the bias. Occasionally, I'll

Approximate size:
20 × 30 inches as illustrated

PLAIN ST. NICK
WALL HANGING

splurge on bias-cut ruffles because they do turn corners more gracefully, but ruffles cut on the straight grain work well if you just gather the corners fully.

Gathering. The method shown here does not require sewing the ruffle into a circle and making it fit a pillow. (A method like that was shown for the Ruffled Napkin on page 26.) This method is easier and more flexible. Gathering is done with the ruffle material in one long strip; press the strip in half and gather both layers at once.

The prettiest ruffles are gathered with two rows of machine basting, approximately ³⁄₁₆ inch apart. The double row of stitching gives better control when you pull the fabric up on the threads as well as when sewing the ruffle to the pillow top. This is why the ½-inch seam allowance is nice. Sewing ruffles to a pillow top when you have only ¼-inch seam allowance is, at best, a difficult and frustrating task.

An alternate way to ruffle that is almost as attractive as and a lot quicker than the double rows of gathering is to lay down a wide zigzag stitch over a small string, then gather the fabric on the string. Try not to stitch on the string when sewing the ruffle in place so the string can be removed.

Attaching ruffles. When the ruffles are gathered, pin them to the pillow top, raw edges matching and with the right side of the ruffle laying on the pillow. Start pinning at the center of one side, not a corner. Adjust the fullness around the pillow. Be sure to allow extra fullness around the corners. When the ruffle is pinned all around the pillow, fold back both raw edges and overlap the ends so that no raw edges will be visible from the front (Figure 1). Baste or pin the overlap in place.

Types of Ruffles

Single ruffle. In my opinion, one layer of fabric with gathering on one edge and a narrow hem on the other edge is too skimpy unless it is on top of another ruffle. Therefore, my single ruffles are cut twice as wide as the desired finished width plus two seam allowances. The strip is folded in half lengthwise and the raw edges stitched together by gathering.

Double ruffles. Two single ruffles of varying widths stacked one atop the other. When stacking ruffles, reduce their fullness to 1¾ times the perimeter of the pillow as the gathered thicknesses get very bulky.

Mock double ruffle. This is a clever way to save fabric and reduce bulk in the pillow seam. Determine the desired width of the top ruffle of a double ruffle. Cut the strip that wide plus two seam allowances. Figure how wide you want the second ruffle; *subtract* from this the *finished* width of the first ruffle. Seam the strips together, fold the fabric in half and proceed as for a single ruffle. You can insert lace or other trim in this seam (Figure 2).

Mock triple ruffle. Like a mock double ruffle, but it has a third fabric.

Purchased trims. Some are very lovely and even though they may seem expensive, if you calculate the time and materials for the ones you make, they are usually a good investment.

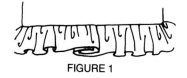

FIGURE 1

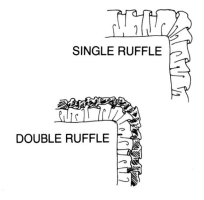

SINGLE RUFFLE

DOUBLE RUFFLE

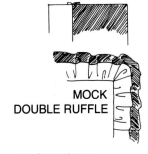

MOCK
DOUBLE RUFFLE

LACE INSERT

FIGURE 2

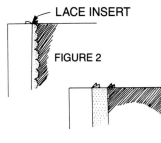

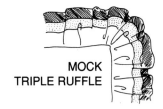

MOCK
TRIPLE RUFFLE

Starry Night Ruffle Measurements

Each pillow, like each wall hanging or other project, will be uniquely yours because your fabrics and trims are different, but here is a brief explanation of how each star pillow was finished.

After the patchwork was completed, 1½-inch-wide border strips were added to all the pillows to center the star(s) on top of the pillows. Without that extra strip, the outside edge of the patchwork tends to disappear in the curvature of the pillow. Different fabric designs and colors may look better with different widths of strips.

Star "A" pillow (photo, bottom left) has a double ruffle. The first ruffle has a finished width of 1¼ inches; the second ruffle is 2 inches wide.

Star "B" pillow and Star "D" pillow (photo, top left) are finished like a matching pair, even though the patchwork is different. Both have a mock double ruffle with an insert. The insert is a simple flap of fabric; because it is fabric, not lace or eyelet, at first glance it may look like it is a narrow strip of fabric seamed on each side to another fabric.

For the flap, a 1-inch-wide strip was cut on the straight grain, folded in half, and inserted into the seam between the first and second ruffle fabrics. The finished width of the whole ruffle is 1¾ inches. The first ruffle section has a finished width of 1 inch; the second extends ¾ inch beyond the first, but the flap covers ¼ inch of it.

Star "C" pillow (photo, top right) combines four small patchwork stars, adding needed strips of background fabric to make them into a square. It is finished with a mock double ruffle. The first section of the ruffle is 1½ inches finished and the second is ½ inch.

Star "E" pillow (photo, bottom right) has a mock triple ruffle. The *finished* visible widths are 1 inch for the navy and ½ inch for both of the other fabrics.

Pillow Finishing

Good quality polyester stuffing eliminates the need to make removable pillow covers. Just be sure you're using washable stuffing. A layer of low-loft batting under the top (even if it is not quilted) will help hide stuffing lumps.

The pillow back should be the same size as the pillow top. Measure your finished pillow top before cutting the back to make sure you have the proper size back and seam allowances for ruffles. Lay the back atop the pillow top, right sides together. Ruffles or piping should already be basted to the top and will lay between top and back. Sew around all sides, leaving a 4- to 5-inch opening. Turn the pillow right side out through the opening.

Use a blunt-pointed object (pencil or crochet hook) to poke out corners and to push in stuffing. Stuff the pillow firmly, making it fuller than really seems right, as stuffing tends to settle and flatten with time. Close opening with a tiny, invisible hand stitch.

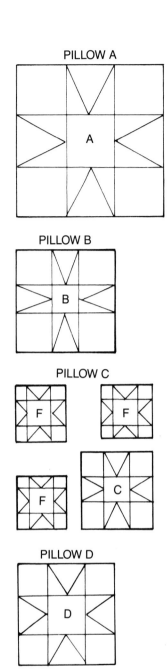

PILLOW A

PILLOW B

PILLOW C

PILLOW D

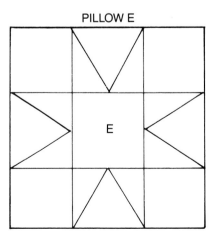

PILLOW E

Christmas Rag Dolls

Approximate size:
7¼ to 8 inches

MATERIALS NEEDED:
Fabric scraps
Stuffing

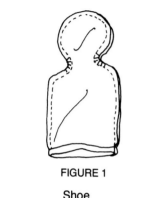

FIGURE 1

Shoe

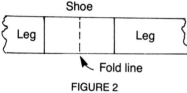

← Fold line

FIGURE 2

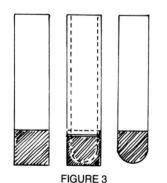

FIGURE 3

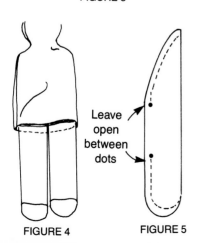

Leave
open
between
dots

FIGURE 4   FIGURE 5

The Old St. Nick and the Victorian-style Angel rag dolls are appropriate for an antique Christmas theme. They can be used as tree ornaments, decoratively on small wreaths, or as traditional toys.

Mark traced patterns for each doll carefully; they may look the same but the Old St. Nick body pieces are larger.

Old St. Nick is featured with contrasting shoes; his legs are cut from the same fabric as his coat and hood.

Making the Body and Head (Both Dolls)

1. Using the appropriate body/head pattern, cut two pieces of flesh-colored fabric for each doll. Use a permanent pen, such as a fine-tipped Pigma™ pen, to trace the face pattern onto the right side of one head piece. Or, use a water-soluble pen if you intend to embroider the features after completing the doll.

2. With right sides together, stitch body/head pieces together. Leave the bottom edge open. Carefully clip all curves.

3. Turn a ¼-inch hem to the inside of the bottom edge (Figure 1).

4. Turn the doll right side out. Stuff the body firmly.

Making the Legs and Feet (Both Dolls)

1. Separate patterns are given for legs and feet so they can be made from contrasting fabrics to create the effect of shoes. To make legs with separate shoes, cut four legs and two shoes for each body. For matching feet and legs, just overlap the patterns, match seam lines, and cut as one piece to eliminate a seam. (Note the shoe/boot patterns are cut on the fold.)

2. Sew a leg to *both* short ends of each shoe piece (Figure 2).

3. Fold shoe piece on fold line, right sides together, matching leg pieces. Stitch down both sides of each leg and shoe combination. Leave open at leg tops. This makes square-bottomed feet as shown in Figure 3. For rounded feet, round the corners at the bottom of each shoe when stitching, then trim the extra fabric.

4. Turn legs right side out and stuff firmly. Stitch the opening shut. (It is not necessary to turn under a seam allowance here.)

5. Insert legs side by side into body opening, making sure legs are even in length. Hand-sew legs to back side of body bottom (Figure 4), then to front.

Making Old St. Nick's Arms

1. For the Old St. Nick doll, use the generic doll arm pattern to cut two arm pieces from flesh-colored fabric.

2. Fold each arm piece with right sides together. Stitch each arm piece around the hand up to the first dot, then sew from the narrow shoulder down to the other dot. Leave open between dots (Figure 5).

3. Trim seam allowances to ⅛ inch; turn right side out. When clipping and trimming seam allowances, *do not* clip and trim the sections between dots that are left open for turning. These openings will be hand-stitched closed later, and a ¼-inch seam allowance is necessary for ease when hand stitching.

4. For each hand, pinch a blueberry-sized piece of stuffing into a ball and poke it into the rounded end of the arm. Match hand sizes carefully. Tie heavy thread around the "wrist" to hold the stuffing in place.

5. Stuff each arm loosely from the hand up to the elbow. Close the opening in the arm, and tie off tightly at the elbow. The arm is not stuffed above the elbow.

6. The folded (unseamed) edge is the top of the arm. Place one arm across the back shoulder (Figure 6). Starting ½ inch from the tip, stitch the arm in place on the bottom side, around the tip, and along the top edge of the arm to the shoulder. Position and stitch the arm on the opposite side in the same manner.

Making the Angel's Arms

1. The angel's arms are made from one piece; cut one for each angel from flesh-colored fabric.

2. Fold the arm piece right sides together and stitch, leaving an opening between dots. Turn and stuff each end lightly. Do not stuff the center section. Close the center opening.

3. Tie a knot in the center of the arm piece for hands (Figure 7).

4. Hand-stitch one tip of the arm piece to the back of one shoulder of the angel body, almost at the nape of the neck as shown in Figure 8. The other end is threaded out one dress sleeve and up the other sleeve, and is not sewn to the shoulder until the doll is dressed.

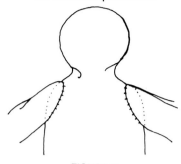

St. Nick arm placement

FIGURE 6

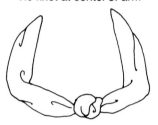

Tie knot at center of arm

FIGURE 7

Arms meet at nape of neck

FIGURE 8

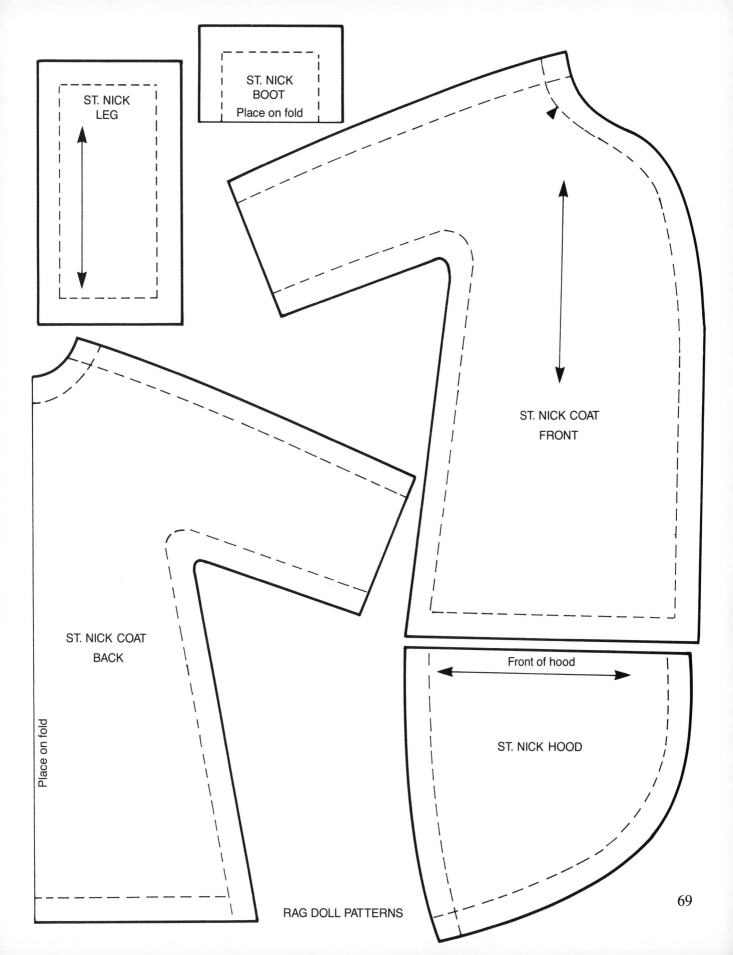

ST. NICK
LEG

ST. NICK
BOOT

Place on fold

ST. NICK COAT
FRONT

ST. NICK COAT
BACK

Place on fold

Front of hood

ST. NICK HOOD

RAG DOLL PATTERNS

69

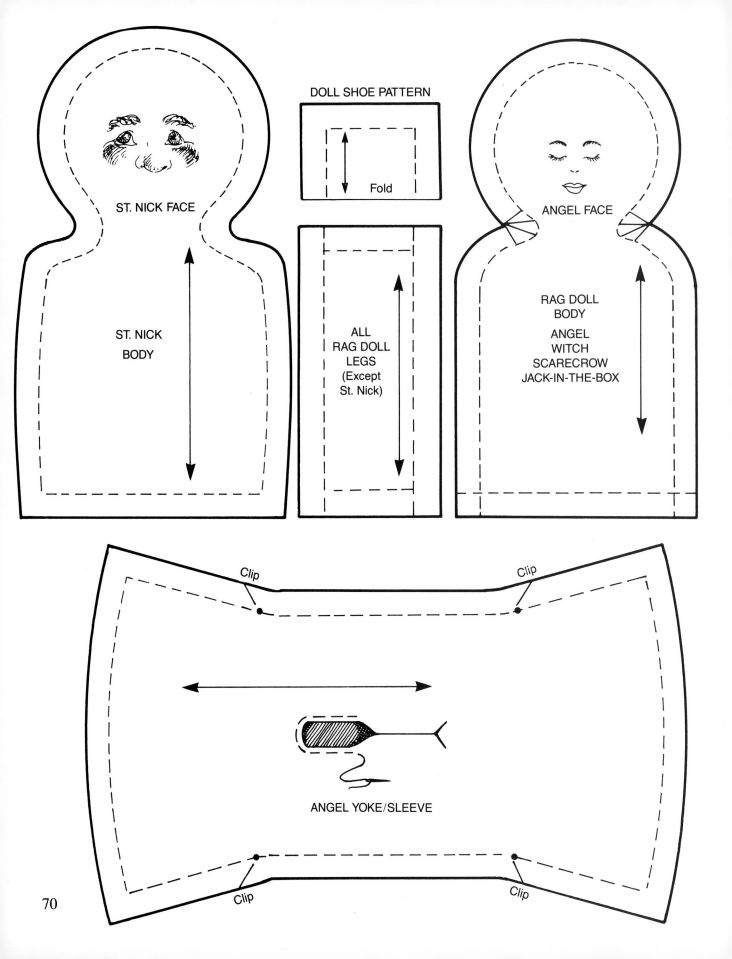

ST. NICK FACE

ST. NICK
BODY

DOLL SHOE PATTERN

Fold

ALL
RAG DOLL
LEGS
(Except
St. Nick)

ANGEL FACE

RAG DOLL
BODY

ANGEL
WITCH
SCARECROW
JACK-IN-THE-BOX

Clip

Clip

ANGEL YOKE/SLEEVE

Clip

Clip

70

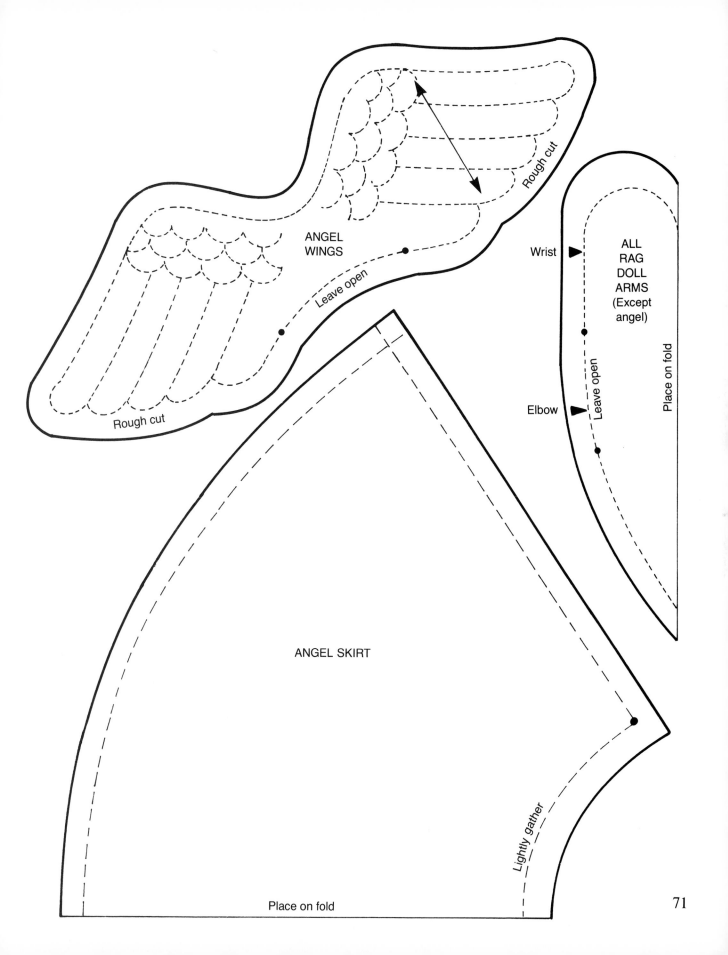

ANGEL WINGS

Rough cut

Rough cut

Leave open

Wrist

Elbow

ALL
RAG
DOLL
ARMS
(Except
angel)

Leave open

Place on fold

ANGEL SKIRT

Lightly gather

Place on fold

71

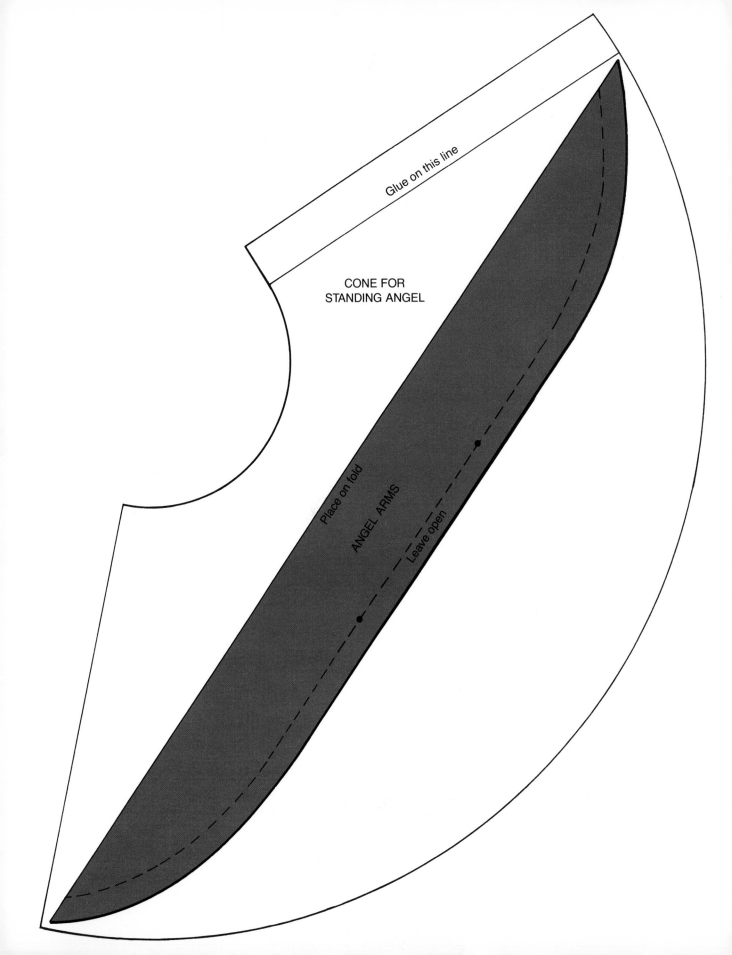

Glue on this line

CONE FOR
STANDING ANGEL

Place on fold

ANGEL ARMS

Leave open

Making the Hair

There are wonderful packaged doll hairs available in craft stores today that contribute realism and personality to each doll. The hair can be glued or stitched in place. Because each is different, experiment a little. Yarn scraps can also be used.

The Doll Clothes

Making Old St. Nick's Coat with Hood

1. Cut two coat fronts, one coat back, and two hood pieces.

2. Stitch coat fronts to back at shoulders. Turn coat right side out.

3. Stitch right sides of hood pieces together around long curved edge. Clip and trim seam allowances. Turn hood right side out so that seam is in center of hood, running from front to back (Figure 1). Press to hold in place.

4. Gather bottom edge of hood. Stitch hood to neck edge of coat between dots. Press seam allowance toward coat.

5. Press under a ¼-inch hem on both sleeves and all around the curved neck and front edges of the coat. Stitch hems in place.

6. If you have fur scraps, you might prefer to make the whole coat, then cut fur strips and stitch or glue them in place. The "fur" on my doll's coat is scrap wool worsted, but muslin would give the same effect. Cut a 1¼ × 15½-inch piece of trim fabric for the coat. Fold the strip in half lengthwise with wrong sides together. Pin trim in place on the right side of the coat's front and neck edges, matching the raw edges of the trim with the hemmed edge of the coat. Stitch in place.

7. To cover the raw seam, pull the folded edge of the trim so it overlaps (but does not wrap around) the hemmed edge of the coat. Slip-stitch in place.

8. For the the cuff, cut a 1 × 3-inch scrap of fur fabric. Baste under ¼ inch along one long edge. With right sides together, stitch the single raw edge of trim to the hemmed edge of the sleeve (Figure 2). Fold the basted edge of the trim to overlap (but not wrap around) the edge of the sleeve. Slip-stitch hemmed edge in place (Figure 3).

9. With right sides together, stitch side and underarm seams of coat. You may wish to hand-stitch the seam allowance of the cuffs down tightly, or trim, so they don't show.

10. Hem bottom edge of coat. After dressing St. Nick, wrap twine around his middle and loosely knot it for a belt.

Approximate size:
Sized to fit doll

MATERIALS NEEDED
FOR ST. NICK DOLL:
Red fabric scraps for coat
Scraps of white wool worsted, muslin, or fur
20-inch length of twine

MATERIALS NEEDED FOR ANGEL:
Scraps of muslin and fleece (or low-loft batting)
Paper-backed fusible webbing

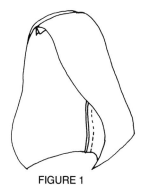

FIGURE 1

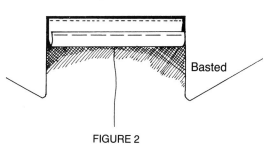

FIGURE 2

Basted

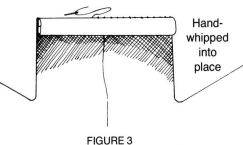

Hand-whipped into place

FIGURE 3

73

Making the Angel's Dress

1. Cut one yoke/sleeve piece. Slash the neck opening as shown on the pattern; do not cut away any fabric as this fabric becomes the neck facing. Turn facing to wrong side along fold lines. Press and, if necessary, baste facings down to hold them in place.

2. Topstitch a ⅛-inch hem around the neck opening and ¼-inch hem at the sleeves.

3. Cut two skirt pieces on the fold. Gather the top edge of each piece between dots to fit between the dots on the yoke's bottom edge (Figure 4). Stitch skirts to yoke as illustrated; do not sew beyond dots into seam allowances. Press seam allowances toward skirt.

4. With right sides together, stitch underarm seam. Pivot where sleeve meets skirt, and stitch skirt side seam. Clip bodice at underarm (Figure 5). Repeat for opposite side.

5. Hem skirt, keeping it slightly longer than the doll.

6. Put dress over doll's head. Pull free end of arm out through one sleeve, then push it up through the wrist of the other sleeve. Sew arm to body by reaching up through the dress bottom.

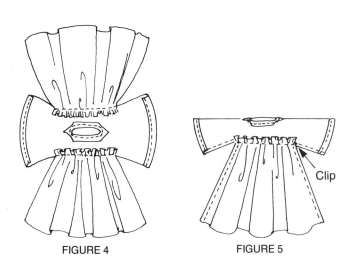

FIGURE 4   FIGURE 5

Clip

Making the Angel's Wing

Use the outside solid line of the wing pattern to cut two layers of muslin. The top of the pattern has an accurate ¼-inch seam allowance that can be used for positioning. The bottom is rough-cut and will be trimmed and clipped after the wing is stitched. The dotted line is the finished size and is the crucial part of the pattern.

1. Trace the finished size wing outline, adding no seam allowances, onto the paper side of rough-cut fusible webbing. Fuse it to fleece. Carefully cut the fused piece on the drawn outline of the wing.

2. Remove the remaining paper from the fusible webbing. Fuse the fleece to the wrong side of one muslin wing piece.

3. On the second muslin wing piece, trace the texture markings from the pattern onto the right side with a disappearing marker.

4. Place the two muslin wings with right sides together. Sewing with the fleece faceup, stitch them together just outside the fleece. Leave an opening between the dots indicated at the bottom of the wing pattern.

5. Carefully clip and trim wing seam allowances. Turn wings right side out; close the opening. Topstitch texture markings onto wings.

6. Hand-stitch wings to center back of dress yoke.

Making a Standing Angel

To make the angel stand, cut the shape of the cone pattern (page 72) from lightweight poster board. Overlap the ends and glue as indicated. The cone fits over the angel's body under the dress and sits flat on a table.

Decorated Feather Trees

These wistful little trees bring to mind the delicate feathered trees of yesteryear and make a perfect background for an Old St. Nick doll. (See photo on page 68).

Making the Button Garland

The buttons used to make my garland were part of a collection. If you haven't been saving or collecting buttons, don't despair. Just look for buttons in muted colors and various sizes. Most of my buttons were cream, tan, and light brown, with some red, green, gold, and blue mixed in for contrast. Diameters range from ¼ inch to ⅞ inch. Fabric stores often have old cards of wonderful buttons for a discounted price such as "10 for $1."

1. Spread your buttons on a large tray or cookie sheet so you can see them all. Sort groups of buttons that please you, putting various sizes, colors, and numbers of buttons in each group.

2. Cut a piece of brown embroidery floss, 18 to 24 inches long. Tie a knot to make a small loop at one end of the floss; place the loop over one of the tree's bottom branches.

3. Thread one group of buttons onto the embroidery floss, then loop the floss around the next branch, letting the buttons hang between the branches. Wind the floss around the branch one or two times to secure it. You may wish to occasionally thread one button on the floss and secure it to the tree branch as you go.

4. Continue threading button groups and looping between boughs as desired. Secure the end of the floss by tying a knotted loop as you did before. Clip excess thread.

Approximate sizes:
Small tree, 11½ inches tall; large tree, 14½ inches tall

MATERIALS NEEDED:
Purchased or homemade artificial trees
Scraps of red print fabric for hearts
Scraps of tan print fabric for stars
Old buttons of varied colors and sizes
Brown embroidery floss
Polyester filling
Thick, clear-drying craft glue

Making the Hanging Buttons

1. Following the directions given for the garland, arrange small groups of buttons.

2. Thread each group onto a length of brown embroidery floss.

3. Leaving a 1½-inch-long loop above the buttons, tie a square knot. Tie a small bow above the square knot; trim ends of floss.

4. Hang button groups on tree as desired.

Making the Stars and Small Hearts

1. The stars and hearts were made using the Line and Turn for Appliqué method (see page 21). Using the patterns given below, make one star and several hearts of each tree. Stitch, turn, and stuff lightly.

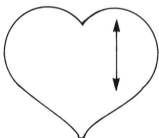

2. Whip the slit closed on the back of each star and heart.

3. To conceal the slit and stitches, sew a button onto the front of each shape. When you sew the button on, leave a 3-inch-long tail of thread when you first go into the star from the back. When you are finished sewing the button, do not cut your ending thread coming out the back. Loop these two threads around the branch several times to tie a star to each tree top. Finish with a secure knot; clip threads. You may wish to secure your knot with a dab of glue.

4. To make the loop hanger for the hearts, thread brown embroidery floss (all six strands) onto a needle. Insert the needle into the seam at the top of the heart on one side of the center; push the needle out on the other side, through the seam. Make a loop about 1 inch long; tie a knot. Dab the knot with a bit of clear-drying glue to secure it. Trim the floss ends and hang hearts on the tree as desired.

No-Sew Stacking or Nesting Boxes

Directions are given for making a 5-inch square box. If making a smaller size, use the appropriate cutting measurements given in the chart, opposite.

1. Cut five 5-inch squares from heavy cardboard for the box sides and bottom. Cut an 11 × 21-inch piece of fabric to cover the outside of the box.

Approximate sizes:
5 inches, 4¼ inches, 3½ inches, 2¾ inches, and 2 inches square

MATERIALS NEEDED:
Extra-thick crafts glue
Stiff, heavy cardboard
Fabric for covering and lining
   each box
Paper-backed fusible webbing
Fabric and batting for padded
   accents (optional)

76

2. On the wrong side of the fabric, arrange the cardboard squares a hair's breadth apart as shown in Figure 1. Allow ½-inch-wide glue flaps on all sides as shown.

3. Glue the left flap onto the two side squares, then glue the top flap. Let the glue dry for a few minutes, then trim the excess fabric at the bottom, leaving ½-inch-wide glue flaps on the new edges. Snip diagonally into the inside corner (Figure 2).

4. Glue all remaining fabric edges to the cardboard except for the one on the right in Figure 2. This flap will be used when folding and securing the squares into a box.

5. For the box lining, trace the outside edges of the square assembly (including the loose flap) onto the wrong side of lining fabric. Cut just inside the marked line. Using paper-backed fusible webbing, fuse the lining to the square assembly and flap.

6. Referring to Figure 3, fold four squares into a box, letting the remaining section hang free. Glue the wrong side of the loose flap to the adjacent inside edge as shown. Complete the box by folding the fifth square into place and gluing the edges (Figure 4).

Box Size—Cut Fabric
2 inches—5 × 9 inches
2¾ inches—6½ × 12 inches
3½ inches—8 × 15 inches
4¼ inches—9½ × 18 inches
5 inches—11 × 21 inches

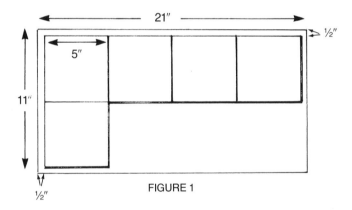

FIGURE 1

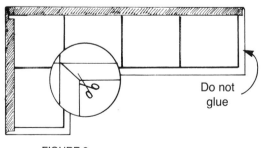

Do not glue

FIGURE 2

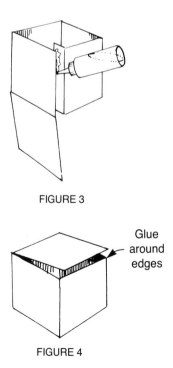

FIGURE 3

Glue around edges

FIGURE 4

7. If padded accents are desired, cut from one to four cardboard and batting squares approximately ¾ inch smaller than the box squares. Cut fabric squares 1 inch larger (for ½-inch glue flaps all around) than those cardboard squares. Layer batting and fabric atop these cardboard squares; pull the fabric over the cardboard edges and glue all edges down. Glue padded accents onto the sides of your finished box as desired.

Stacked Box Alternatives

You can accent a box with cross-stitch, Christmas cards, or any number of things. One illustrated idea shows four boxes the same size made to look like child's blocks, spelling out a message or a name. The other shows three boxes of different sizes stacked and wrapped with a pretty bow and greenery.

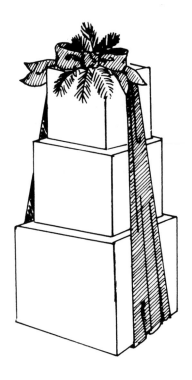

Jack-in-the-Box

Approximate size:

6½ inches tall in a 2-inch-square
  box

MATERIALS NEEDED:

Extra-thick crafts glue
Cardboard
Fabric for covering and lining
  the box
Scraps of muslin, Christmas
  prints, and satin
Paper-backed fusible webbing
20 inches of rickrack
One ⅜-inch-diameter pom-pom
Embroidery floss for facial
  features
Batting and fabric for padded
  accents (optional)

Making Jack

Use the angel's head/body and the generic rag doll arm patterns (Chapter 3) to make Jack, as well as the face, collar, and hat patterns below. The shirt pattern (also used for the Halloween Scarecrow Doll) is on page 128. Don't worry about a leg pattern because Jack has no legs.

1. Follow the directions for the St. Nick Doll's head/body and arms on page 66 to make Jack's head/body and arms. Sew the arms to the center back as for the angel doll, referring to Figure 8 on page 67. When the body is complete, whip the bottom closed.

2. Make Jack's shirt from a Christmas print fabric, following the directions for the Scarecrow's shirt on page 128, except do not add burlap trim. Put shirt on Jack.

3. Fuse two 4-inch squares of satin together, with wrong sides together. From this layered fabric, cut one collar. Gently work the collar over Jack's head to his neck.

4. Cut one hat from the Christmas fabric and one from muslin for lining. Stitch these right sides together, leaving an opening between dots. Clip and

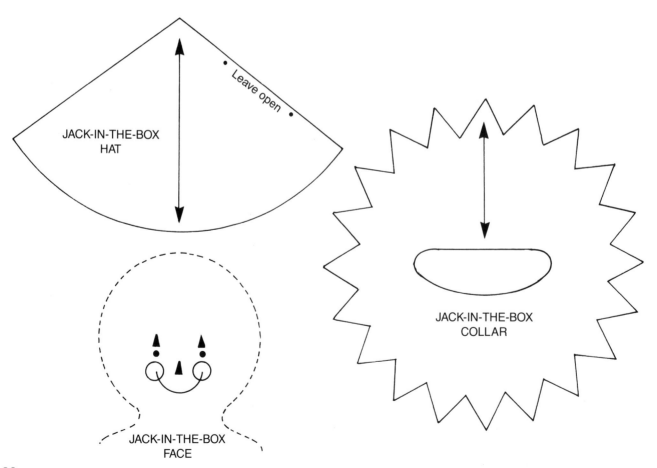

JACK-IN-THE-BOX
HAT

Leave open

JACK-IN-THE-BOX
FACE

JACK-IN-THE-BOX
COLLAR

trim seam allowances, then turn the hat right side out. Slip-stitch the opening. Stitch hat to Jack's head.

5. For the hat band, cut a ¾ × 5-inch piece of satin on the bias. Fold both raw edges into the middle, making the band ⅜ inch wide, and whip those edges together. Position the band with one edge ⅛ inch from the edge of the hat and right sides together (Figure 1). Stitching near the bottom edge, sew the band to the hat and head. Roll the band down, covering the raw edges, and tack it in place. Fold the tip of the hat down, and tack it in place. Glue pom-pom on tip of hat.

6. For the top collar, hand-stitch a gathering thread along each side of the rickrack as shown in Figure 2. With the ends of the rickrack at the back of Jack's neck, pull the gathering threads to fit the ricktack atop Jack's satin collar. Pull the top thread more tightly than the bottom thread in order to make the rickrack lie flat (Figure 3). Tie the ends of the top gathering thread together, then tie the ends of the bottom gathering thread. If necessary, use thread to bind off the rickrack's raw ends and to tack the top collar to Jack's neck.

7. Using the pattern on page 76, cut two heart pieces. Stitch right sides together; slit the back side of one heart to turn the right side out. Stuff the heart lightly, then whip the back slit shut. Tack the heart between Jack's hands.

8. Embroider Jack's eyes and mouth. Embellish his face with fine-tipped permanent pens.

Making Jack's Box

This box is made in the same manner as the Stacking Boxes, with an extra cardboard square used to make a box top.

1. Cut six 2-inch squares from heavy cardboard for the sides, bottom, and lid of the box. Cut a 7 × 9-inch piece of fabric to cover the box.

2. Referring to Figure 1, arrange the cardboard squares a hair's breadth apart on the wrong side of the fabric, allowing for ½-inch-wide glue flaps. Glue the fabric to the cardboard across one end with two squares (Figure 2). Let glue dry a few minutes.

3. Trim the excess fabric on one side as shown in Figure 2, leaving a ½-inch glue flap along the edge. Snip diagonally into the inside corner, then glue edges in place. Trim and glue the opposite side in the same manner.

4. Snip the glue flap to the edge of the cardboard between the two remaining unglued squares at the bottom of the assembly. Glue the right side down as shown in Figure 3. The remaining flap will be used when folding and securing the box.

5. Complete the box lining in the same manner as for the Stacking Boxes (page 77).

6. Fold the box into a square with a lid. Glue the wrong side of the loose flap to the inside adjacent edge; secure the bottom of the box with glue.

7. Put Jack in the box. It may be necessary to put a little stuffing in the bottom of the box to hold him in the proper position.

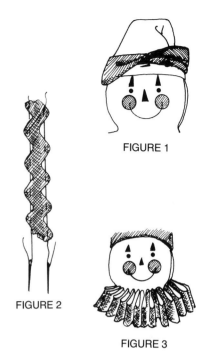

FIGURE 1

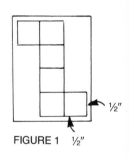

FIGURE 2

FIGURE 3

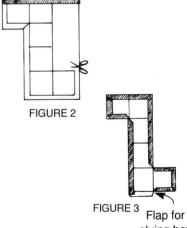

FIGURE 1   ½″

FIGURE 2

FIGURE 3   Flap for gluing box together

Bear Foot Stockings

Approximate size:

9 inches tall

MATERIALS NEEDED:

10×14-inch pieces of fabric and lining for each stocking

10×14-inch piece of Thermore™ or other low-loft batting

Fabric scraps for cuff, facing, and desired appliqué

Assorted ribbons

Purchased bumblebee appliqués (optional)

These small stockings are perfect for pets (don't forget A. Bear, there is one for him, too) or for holiday decorations. Reinforce the pet theme by using printed fabrics with dog, cat, and bear motifs.

1. Use the leg/foot pattern (page 43) from A. Bear for All Seasons. For each stocking, cut one piece from stocking fabric, lining, and batting. Note that the back of the leg is cut on the fold.

2. Layer fabric, batting, and lining with right sides of fabric and lining showing. Pin the layers together, matching raw edges.

3. Use the stocking outline around each appliqué design on pages 84 and 85 as a positioning guide. Cut appliqué pieces and machine-appliqué through all three layers. Use a very narrow zigzag stitch for the detail lines. An alternate method would be to fuse the designs in place, using fabric paint for the outline and details.

4. Cut two cuff pieces. Sew them together, leaving the straight side open. Clip and trim seam allowances. Turn cuff right side out; press.

5. Matching raw edges, lay cuff on the right side of stocking body between the side seam allowances (Figure 1). Stitch cuff to stocking.

6. From lining fabric, cut one $3 \times 8\frac{3}{4}$-inch facing piece (includes seam allowance). Stitch a ¼-inch hem along one long edge. With raw edges even and right sides together, stitch facing to stocking.

7. Press the facing up, then press the seam allowance down toward the stocking (Figure 2).

8. With facing still turned up, fold stocking in half on center back line, right sides together. Stitch around the raw edges, leaving the top open (Figure 3). Clip and trim seam allowances; turn stocking right side out. Tuck the facing inside the stocking.

9. Add ribbon trim to front of stocking. Make a small ribbon loop at center back for hanging.

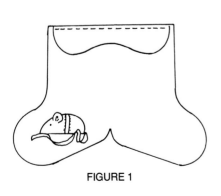

FIGURE 1

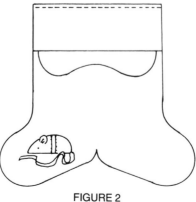

FIGURE 2

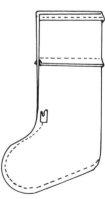

FIGURE 3

MOUSE EAR

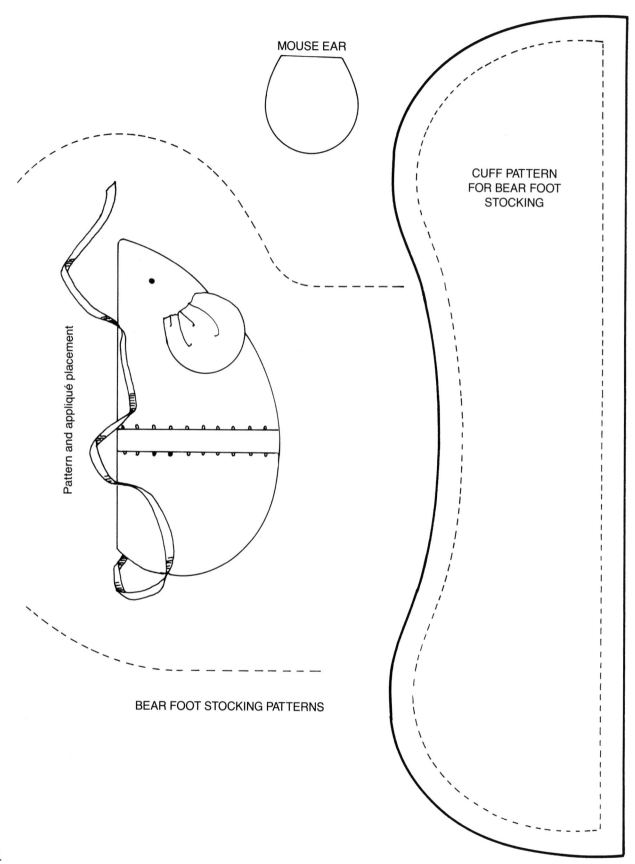

CUFF PATTERN
FOR BEAR FOOT
STOCKING

Pattern and appliqué placement

BEAR FOOT STOCKING PATTERNS

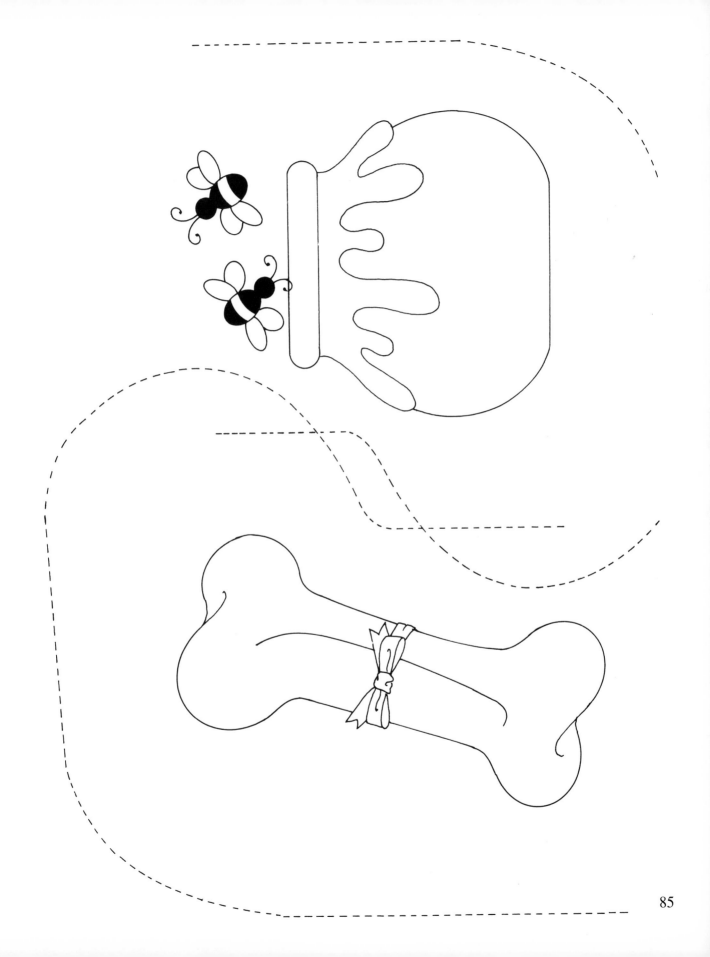

Approximate size:
25 inches tall

MATERIALS NEEDED:
⅝ yard of 60-inch-wide or ⅞
  yard of 45-inch-wide red wool
  fabric for A. Bear body
Scrap of Valentine print fabric
  for collar
Lining fabric for collar
Scrap of red chintz for heart
Polyester filling
58 inches of 1-inch-wide
  gathered lace
48-inch lengths of assorted
  narrow ribbons
Heart-shaped buttons, ⅜- to
  ⅞-inch widths

CHAPTER SIX

VALENTINE'S DAY

Valentine A. Bear with Sweetheart Collar

Making Valentine A. Bear
Follow the directions in Chapter 4 to make Valentine A. Bear's body from red wool fabric.

Making the Sweetheart Collar
  1. Use the Pilgrim Collar back pattern on page 147 to cut four collar pieces on the fold from Valentine print fabric, and four pieces from lining

fabric. (The front collar piece is not used here.) Stitch collar pieces together for both collar and lining (Figure 1).

2. Baste gathered lace to the bottom edge of the collar (Figure 2). Turn back raw ends.

3. Stitch collar and lining together, leaving an opening at back inside edge for turning. Turn collar right side out. Slip-stitch the opening and press.

4. Gather inside edge of collar with a running stitch. Fit collar around A. Bear's neck and adjust gathers.

5. Cut two heart pieces. Referring to the Line and Turn technique on page 20, make a stuffed heart. Hand-stitch the remaining gathered lace to the back of the stuffed heart (Figure 3). This lace is not stitched into the seam because it is hard to accomplish successfully with the small heart shape and wide lace.

6. Use 13-inch lengths of ⅛-inch-wide ribbons to make a bow for the stuffed heart. Tack the bow in place with a ⅞-inch-wide heart button.

7. Use 24-inch lengths of assorted ribbons to tie in a bow around A. Bear's ear. Tack the bow in place and add heart-shaped buttons.

Variations on Valentine A. Bear

See page 95 to see how another bear dresses for Valentine's Day.

For a feminine Valentine A. Bear, dress the white wool St. Patrick's A. Bear in a vest (page 45) made from a feminine fabric. Gather tulle to fit the bottom of the vest for a skirt, and the shoulders for cap sleeves. Add a lace bosom inset in deference to Miss A. Bear's modesty.

Create a beautiful Christmas look with the red bear and a green velvet vest with a white satin collar.

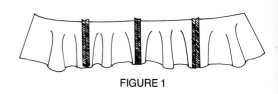

FIGURE 1

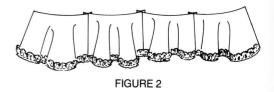

FIGURE 2

FIGURE 3

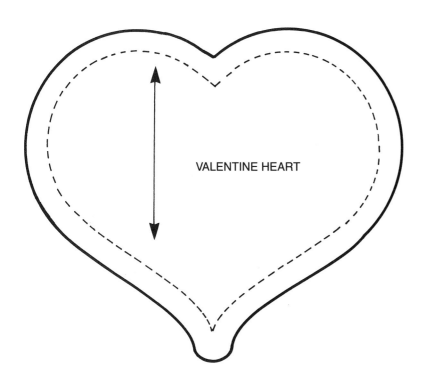

VALENTINE HEART

VALENTINE A. BEAR

Shirred Heart Pillow

This pillow showcases a technique called shirring. Shirring is an attractive, romantic addition to pillows and small quilts. It is easy to do, but takes a little practice and patience. Shirring is done by gathering both sides of a strip or inset. The hardest part is to gather evenly to maintain an orderly appearance. The perimeter of the shirred inset on this heart-shaped pillow is longer on one side than the other, which requires extra patience.

Making the Pillow Top

1. Trace the large heart, matching notches to connect the two parts of the pattern. Using your traced pattern, cut one heart for the pillow front and one for the back. Cut two hearts of fleece; baste one fleece heart to the wrong side of each fabric heart.

2. Cut two 4 × 45-inch strips of lace fabric for the shirred inset. Stitch these strips together at short edges, making a circle.

3. Run two rows of machine basting ¼ inch apart on *both* sides of the strip; gather evenly to approximately 38½ inches.

4. With right side up, pin the outside edge of the gathered inset to the outside edge of the heart. Match inset seams with points of heart. Adjust gathers. When outside is smooth and even and securely basted or pinned in place, work on the inside edge. Topstitch the inner edge only (Figure 1).

5. Use the small heart pattern on page 91 to cut one heart of appliqué fabric and one of fleece. Lining the appliqué with the fleece, stay-stitch ¼ inch from the raw edge of the appliqué. Trim and clip the curves and inward corner of the seam allowance, then press the raw edges under.

6. Center the appliqué faceup on the pillow, overlapping the inset. Slip-stitch it in place, leaving an opening to insert stuffing (Figure 2). Stuff appliqué firmly, then slip-stitch the opening.

Making the Ruffles

1. Cut two 4½ × 45-inch strips for the ruffle and stitch them together into one long strip. Fold the ruffle strip in half lengthwise with wrong sides together and baste raw edges together. Gather the ruffle to approximately 38½ inches.

2. Cut a 38½-inch length of the pregathered lace. Stitch the gathered edge of the lace to the raw edge of the ruffle, turning under the ends of the lace.

3. Pin ruffle to pillow, right sides together, adjusting the gathers to fit (Figure 3). Baste ruffle in place.

Completing the Pillow

Pin pillow back to front, right sides together, over the ruffle. Stitch, taking a ½-inch-wide seam allowance and leaving an opening for turning. Clip seam allowance curves and inward corner. Cut the bottom point diagonally (Figure 4). Turn pillow right side out; stuff firmly. Slip-stitch the opening shut (Figure 5).

Approximate size:

15½ inches

MATERIALS NEEDED:
½ yard of red fabric for pillow and heart appliqué
½ yard of lace fabric for shirred inset
¼ yard of ruffle fabric
1⅛ yards of 1½-inch-wide red pregathered lace
Thermore™ or fleece
Polyester filling

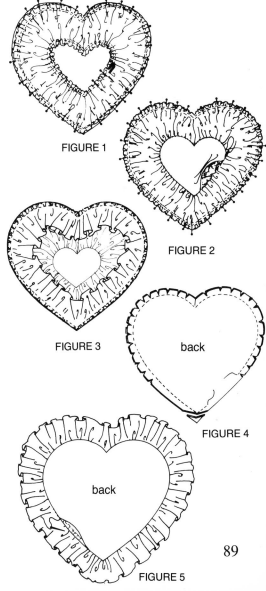

FIGURE 1

FIGURE 2

FIGURE 3

back

FIGURE 4

back

FIGURE 5

89

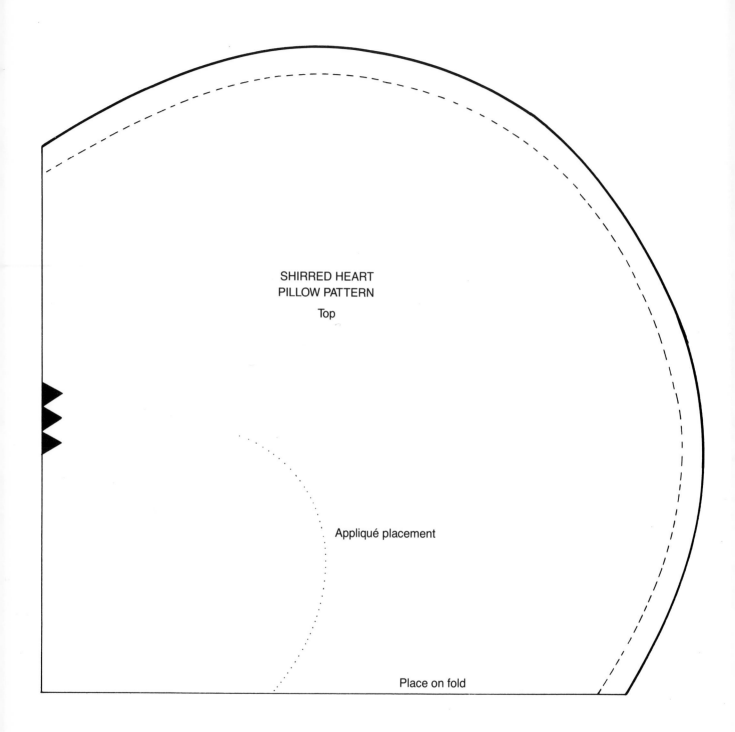

SHIRRED HEART
PILLOW PATTERN

Top

Appliqué placement

Place on fold

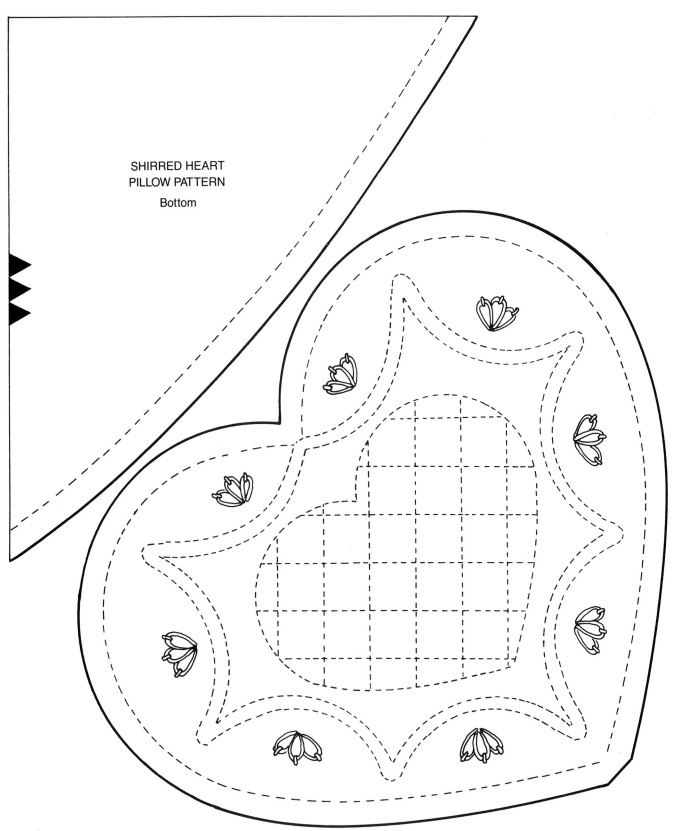

SHIRRED HEART
PILLOW PATTERN
Bottom

HEART TRAPUNTO PILLOW PATTERN
(also appliqué for
shirred pillow)

The World's Easiest Pretty Pillow

Approximate size:
14 × 18 inches

MATERIALS NEEDED:
14 × 40-inch piece of fabric for
    large (bottom) pillow
14 × 32-inch piece of fabric for
    small (top) pillow
5½ × 18-inch piece of fabric for
    center band
Thermore™ or fleece to match
    each fabric piece
Polyester filling

The World's Easiest Pretty Pillow looks romantic enough for a Valentine celebration, but the real beauty of this pillow is its simplicity. You just make two rectangular pillows (one slightly smaller than the other), stack them, and tie them together with a tight fabric band to create a bow effect. For a romantic look, try taffeta, moiré, chintz, velvet, or lined lace fabrics. This pillow also looks great in tapestry fabrics, country plaid, or suitable holiday prints.

Note that any directional fabric design should run parallel to the short dimension of the required rectangles for the pillow pieces and on the long dimension for the band.

Instead of making a matching band for your pillow, consider using a pretty cord or making an elasticized fabric tube like a ponytail holder. Or, add ruffles or lace to both edges of a fabric band.

1. If you are using slippery taffeta fabric, pin or baste matching pieces of fleece and fabric together. This is probably not necessary for other fabrics.

2. For each pillow, fold the fabric in half with the right sides together as shown in Figure 1. Stitch the side seam first, leaving several inches open for turning.

3. Turn the cylinder that you have just created so that the seam is at the center front. Stitch across the top and bottom (Figure 2). Clip corners, then turn the pillow right side out.

4. Lightly stuff both pillows, putting very little stuffing in the middles where they will be bunched by the center band. Slip-stitch the openings. Stack and center the small pillow atop the larger one.

5. Fold the band fabric in half lengthwise with right sides together; stitch long edges of the band together. Turn band right side out. Roll and press the seam to the center of the back side of the band. Turn and press the raw edges of each end to the inside of the band.

6. Wrap the band around pillows, experimenting with the tightness until you like the result (Figure 3). Hand-stitch the ends in place or just tuck the ends under the band for ease in removing it for cleaning.

FIGURE 1

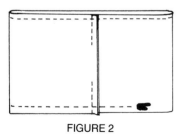

FIGURE 2

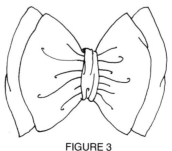

Wrap band tightly around pillows

FIGURE 3

Heart Trapunto Pillow

Trapunto is a decorative form of quilting made by stitching two fabric layers together, then stuffing the stitched area with batting or cording to create a raised surface design. It may be further embellished with embroidery, ribbons, or buttons.

This charming little pillow adds interest to a grouping of larger pillows, or is the perfect size for a potpourri or ring bearer's pillow. All the stitching on this pillow may be done by machine.

1. Using the small heart pattern on page 91, cut two hearts from the pillow fabric, one from muslin, and one from batting.

2. Place one fabric piece over the printed pattern, right side up. Use a water-erasable pen or other removable marker to trace all stitching lines onto the fabric.

3. Sandwich the batting between the marked pillow top and the muslin. Baste the three layers together around the outside edge.

4. Using a small machine stitch, sew through all three layers along the marked lines of the channels and around the outer edge of the center heart (Figure 1). Machine-quilt the cross-hatched lines of the center heart last.

5. Use a tapestry needle and yarn to cord the meandering channels. Make tiny slits in the muslin backing fabric and pull the yarn through the channel (Figure 2). Leave a short tail of yarn extending outside the muslin (Figure 3). Whip the opening shut if necessary.

6. Complete the design by embroidering Lazy Daisy stitches as shown on the pattern.

7. Baste lace around the outside edge of the pillow top.

8. See page 65 for general instructions on pillow finishing.

Approximate size:
9½ × 12 inches

MATERIALS NEEDED:
Two 8-inch squares for pillow top and back
8-inch squares of muslin and batting
30 inches of yarn for trapunto
24 inches of 4-inch-wide pregathered lace for ruffle
Embroidery thread and tapestry needle
Polyester filling
Water-soluble marking pen

FIGURE 1

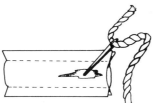

FIGURE 2

FIGURE 3

Approximate size:
25 inches tall

MATERIALS NEEDED:
⅝ yard of 60-inch-wide or ⅞
   yard of 45-inch-wide white
   wool fabric for A. Bear body
½ yard of green satin fabric for
   vest
Sequin trim

CHAPTER SEVEN

ST. PATRICK'S DAY

St. Patrick's A. Bear and Year-Round Holiday Wardrobe

St. Patrick's A. Bear started as a perfect representative of St. Patrick's Day. Once the decision was made to use the white wool gabardine remnant for A. Bear instead of a vest for me, as originally planned, it was hard to decide on dressing it for only one holiday. The green satin vest and sequin trim for St. Patrick's Day was a must—it's the same pattern as the Christmas vest (pages 46–47)—but other outfits kept coming to mind. It was easier to make them all than to make a decision. At right, St. Patrick's A. Bear celebrates all the holidays in style with a wardrobe of clothing and accessories made from the patterns in this book.

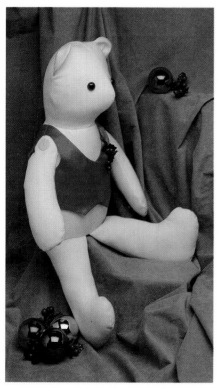

Christmas: A red satin vest and a sprig of holly for his boutonniere put A. Bear in a festive mood.

Valentine's Day: A sophisticated black satin vest with a red rose for his sweetheart. The vest pattern is on pages 46–47.

Easter: A. Bear might not fool anyone, but his Bunny Disguise and bow tie show that he's ready for Easter.

Fourth of July: Decorate A. Bear with patriotic ribbon and purchased gold eagle and stars.

Halloween: Who would know A. Bear in his Yellow Duck disguise? You'll find instructions for the cape in Chapter 10.

Thanksgiving: All dressed for dinner in a Turkey bib. The bib pattern is on page 148.

95

Irish Chain Wall Hanging

Approximate size:
27¼ inches square

MATERIALS NEEDED:
1 yard of light green print fabric
(includes backing)
Scraps or ½ yard of dark green
print fabric (includes outer
border and appliqué)
Scraps or ¼ yard of white fabric
Scraps or ¼ yard of a second
green print fabric for the
inner border
Scraps of paper-backed fusible
webbing
30-inch square of quilt batting

This wall hanging version of a popular quilt design alternates two basic blocks. Crisp green and white fabrics, especially the shamrock print, make a grand St. Patrick's Day welcome for spring. Five blocks are pieced from light and dark prints and white (Block A), and four white blocks have a shamrock appliqué and accented corners (Block B). Each square within the blocks is 1¼ inches finished size.

Cut and set aside a 28-inch square of light green print fabric for the backing. Sew all seams with a ¼-inch seam allowance.

Making Block A

You can cut individual 1¾-inch squares (9 from a dark print, 12 from a light print, and 4 from white) for each Block A, but the strip techniques shown here greatly streamline the process.

1. For rows 1, 2, 4, and 5 (see Figure 1), cut 1¾ × 20-inch strips from the dark green print, light green print, and white fabric. Cut more strips if your scraps are not 20 inches long.

2. For row 3, cut 1¾ × 11-inch strips from each of the three fabrics.

3. Seam the strips together, making three strip sets (Figure 1). Press all seam allowances away from the light green strips.

4. From both long strip sets, cut ten 1¾-inch-wide cross strips. Cut five cross strips from the short strip set.

5. Seam the pieced rows together in the correct order (Figure 2). Complete five of Block A in this manner.

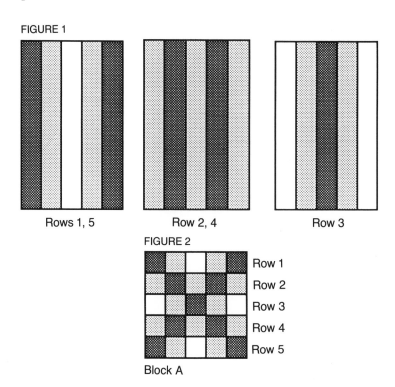

FIGURE 1

Rows 1, 5   Row 2, 4   Row 3

FIGURE 2

Row 1
Row 2
Row 3
Row 4
Row 5

Block A

FIGURE 3

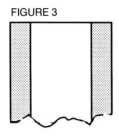

FIGURE 4

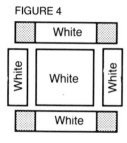

Making Block B

Measure across three adjacent squares in each Block A. They should measure 3¾ inches. If discrepancies in cutting, sewing, or pressing have resulted in a different measurement, then adjust the size of the strips (or squares) to be cut in the next step to the same width as these squares, adding ½ inch for two seam allowances.

1. For strip piecing, cut one 4¼-inch-wide (or adjusted width) strip of white fabric and two 1¾-inch-wide strips of light green print fabric. Cut all the strips the same length. You need 15-inch-long strips or enough length to cut eight cross strips 1¾ inches wide. Using Figure 3 as a guide, piece the strips together; then cut eight cross strips. If not using strip techniques, cut eight 1¾ × 4¼-inch white strips and sixteen 1¾-inch light green print squares.

2. To finish the B blocks, cut eight 1¾ × 4¼-inch strips and four 4¼-inch squares of white fabric.

3. Assemble the strips and squares as shown in Figure 4 to make four of Block B. Press seam allowances toward the white fabric.

4. Cut four shamrocks from fused dark green print fabric. Fuse a shamrock onto the center square of each Block B.

Putting the Blocks Together

Lay the blocks out on the floor, alternating A and B blocks as shown in the Assembly Diagram. Keep the grainlines in the blocks going in the same direction wherever possible. Seam the blocks together.

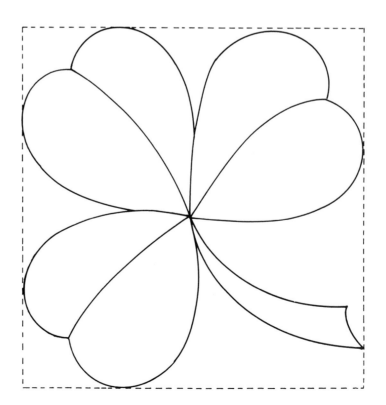

Adding the Borders

Measure your quilt before cutting borders. Border lengths given are mathematically correct, but may not be exact for your quilt.

1. For the inner border, cut two $1\frac{1}{8} \times 19\frac{1}{4}$-inch strips and two $1\frac{1}{8} \times 20\frac{1}{2}$-inch strips. Sew the shorter strips to opposite sides of the quilt, then add the longer borders to the remaining sides.

2. For the middle border, cut four $1\frac{3}{4} \times 20\frac{1}{2}$-inch strips of light green fabric and four $1\frac{3}{4}$-inch squares of dark green print. Sew a square to each end of two border strips. Stitch the shorter borders to the opposite sides of the quilt first. (Always begin adding each successive border to the same pair of opposite sides.) Then add the borders with corner squares to the remaining sides.

3. For the last border, cut four 3×23-inch strips of the dark green print and four 3-inch squares of light green print. Add this last border in the same manner as the middle border.

Finishing the Quilt

This quilted wall hanging is finished in a way slightly different from the traditional method. The quilt top is layered with the pieced backing and the batting, sewn together, and turned right side out.

1. From the remaining light green fabric, cut a right triangle with 12-inch legs. With right sides together, position the triangle at one corner of the backing fabric as shown in Figure 5. Machine-stitch approximately 4 inches in from each end of the diagonal side, leaving an opening as shown. Trim the backing fabric from the seam, leaving a $\frac{1}{4}$-inch seam allowance.

2. Layer batting, quilt top, and backing, with right sides of the top and backing together. Stitch a $\frac{1}{4}$ inch seam all around. Turn the quilt through the opening in the pieced backing. Slip-stitch opening closed.

3. Quilt in the ditch around the borders and between blocks. With a narrow, tight machine zigzag stitch, make accent marks and outline shamrocks. Topstitch $\frac{1}{4}$ inch from the edge of the quilt to give the illusion of a separate binding.

FIGURE 5

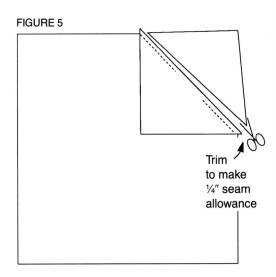

Trim to make $\frac{1}{4}''$ seam allowance

Approximate size:
25 inches tall

MATERIALS NEEDED:
Scrap fabrics for string piecing
⅞ yard of muslin for base
Polyester filling
Purchased eyes and nose
   (optional)
40-inch lengths of narrow
   ribbons in seven assorted
   colors

MATERIALS NEEDED:
Scraps of fabric and fleece for
   hat, lining, and bunny ears
78 inches of ¼-inch-wide ribbon

CHAPTER EIGHT

EASTER

String-Quilted Easter A. Bear

1. Cut all of Easter A. Bear's patterns from muslin, which is used as the base material for string piecing. See page 22 for information on this technique.

2. After string piecing each pattern piece, Easter A. Bear is put together in almost exactly the same manner as the original A. Bear (Chapter 4). It is not necessary to include a fleece lining because the muslin and seam allowances from string piecing provide sufficient extra body.

3. Tie ribbons in a bow around Easter A. Bear's neck. Adjust, and trim ends as desired.

Easter A. Bear's Bunny Disguise

There is something about teddy bears in the springtime that makes them dream of being the Easter Bunny. With a clever ears-in-a-hat disguise, Easter A. Bear pretends to be Easter A. Bunny.

1. Cut four of the back hat pattern (page 104) from the hat fabric and four pieces from Thermore™ or fleece. Baste fleece to the wrong side of all four back hat pieces; treat each basted unit as one piece in the following steps.

2. The ear pattern on page 103 is halved and superimposed on itself to fit the page. Trace one half of the pattern, extend your paper, and trace the remainder of the pattern (Figure 1). Cut four ear pieces.

3. Stitch two ear pieces together all around, leaving the bottom end open. Trim and clip seam allowances, then turn ear right side out. Make second ear in the same manner.

4. Stitch two back hat pieces together at center back; press the seam allowances open. Gather bottom of ears to fit between dots on hat pattern. Matching raw edges, baste ears in place to right side of back hat.

FIGURE 1

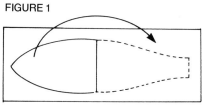

Trace one pattern section, then
flip the paper and trace remaining section

5. Cut one $5\frac{1}{2} \times 18$-inch piece for the front hatband. With right sides together, stitch one long edge of the band to the back hat over the ears (Figure 2).

6. For the back hat lining, stitch two remaining back hat pieces together at center back; press the seam allowances open.

7. Stitch the second raw edge of the front hatband to the lining, right sides together (Figure 3).

8. With hat turned inside out and matching all seams, stitch across the bottom edge of the hat as illustrated in Figure 4, leaving a $\frac{3}{4}$-inch opening at each end. Turn hat right side out and slip-stitch the center opening.

9. Turn in the unstitched seam allowances of the front band and press. Press a fold in the center of the front band. Topstitch $\frac{1}{8}$ inch and $\frac{1}{2}$ inch from the folded edge to make a casing for the ribbon (Figure 5). Thread ribbon through casing. Put the hat on Easter A. Bear and tie a bow under his chin.

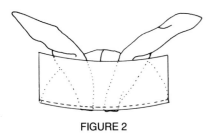

FIGURE 2

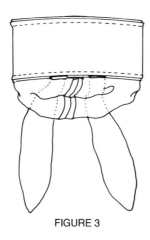

FIGURE 3

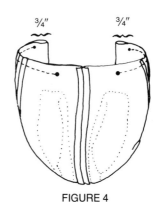

¾"   ¾"

FIGURE 4

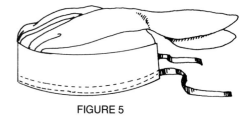

FIGURE 5

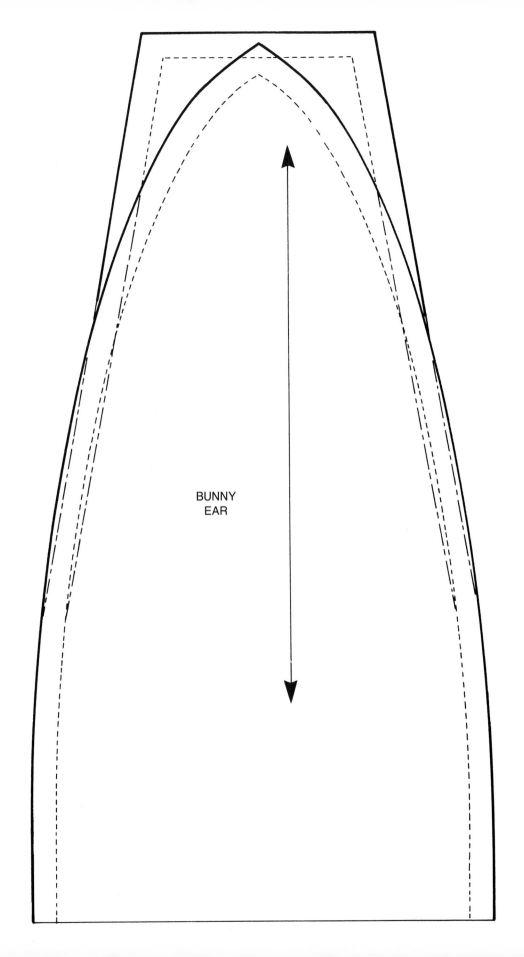

BUNNY
EAR

103

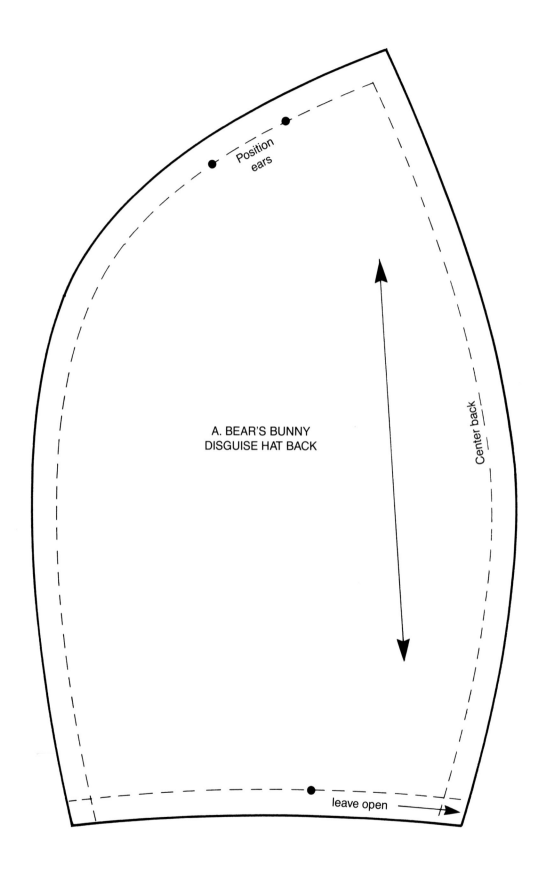

A. BEAR'S BUNNY
DISGUISE HAT BACK

Position
ears

Center back

leave open

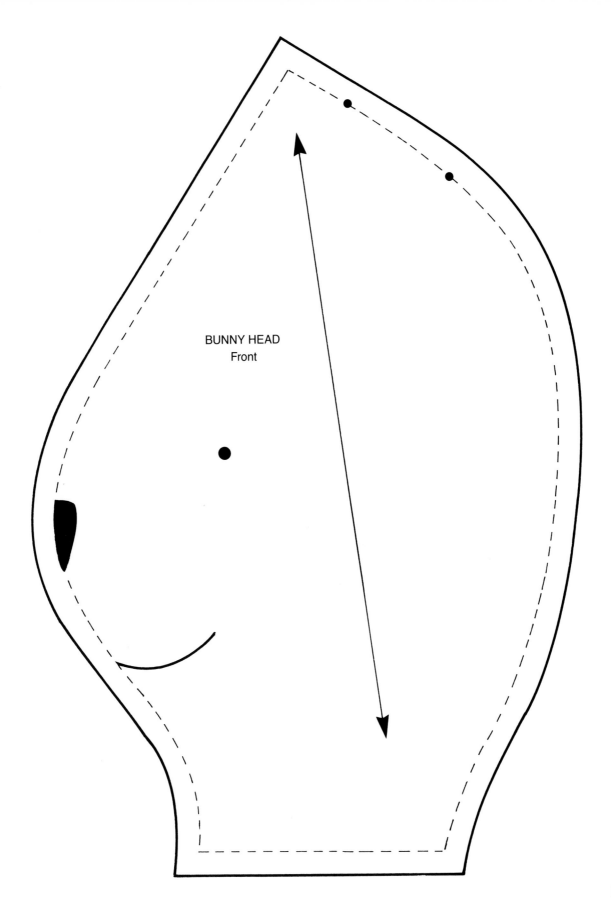

BUNNY HEAD
Front

A. Bunny Variation of A. Bear

Some people won't be fooled by A. Bear in a funny hat—they insist on the real thing! A. Bunny was made from a preprinted quilting fabric, but any pastel print fabric will make a beautiful bunny. A. Bunny can also be string-quilted like Easter A. Bear. Use the same pattern pieces as for A. Bear, substituting the front head pattern on page 105 and the leg and foot patterns on page 108. Use the ear pattern from the Bunny Disguise, page 103.

1. Make A. Bunny's head, arms, and body in the same manner as A. Bear (see Chapter 4).

2. To make the ears, see steps 2 and 3 of Easter A. Bear's Bunny Disguise. Gather the bottom of each ear to fit between dots on the right side of the front head; baste ears in place. Complete head as directed.

3. Cut two legs and two feet pieces. Cut two more feet from heavy interfacing, omitting the seam allowance. Fuse interfacing to fabric feet (Figure 1). Clip seam allowance around each foot to edge of interfacing as shown. Paint or embroider paw markings on feet now.

4. Fold each leg piece and stitch the center front seam from the top edge to the dot at the base of the foot, then stitch the short center back seam between dots. This leaves each leg open at top and bottom. Stuff legs from both ends, making the lower leg very firm. Turn under the lower leg seam allowance. Stay-stitch, if desired, but make sure stitching does not show when edge is turned up.

5. Match center back dot on foot to center back seam of leg. Pin the foot to the leg, adding stuffing as needed, and matching center front dot on foot to center front seam of leg. Blind-stitch the foot in place (Figure 2).

6. Complete the legs and the remainder of A. Bunny in the same manner as for A. Bear, Chapter 4.

7. Tie 44-inch lengths of assorted ribbons in a bow around A. Bunny's neck. Tie 26-inch lengths of ribbon around the base of his ears. Trim ends of ribbon as desired.

Approximate size:
25 inches

MATERIALS NEEDED:
⅝ yard of 60-inch-wide fabric or ⅞ yard of 45-inch-wide fabric

Thermore™ or fleece

Polyester filling

44- and 26-inch lengths of ⅛- to ⅜-inch ribbons in assorted Easter colors

Heavy fusible interfacing

½-inch- and ¾-inch-diameter buttons for eyes

Purchased nose (optional)

Embroidery floss or fabric paint for paw prints (optional)

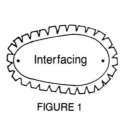

FIGURE 1

FIGURE 2

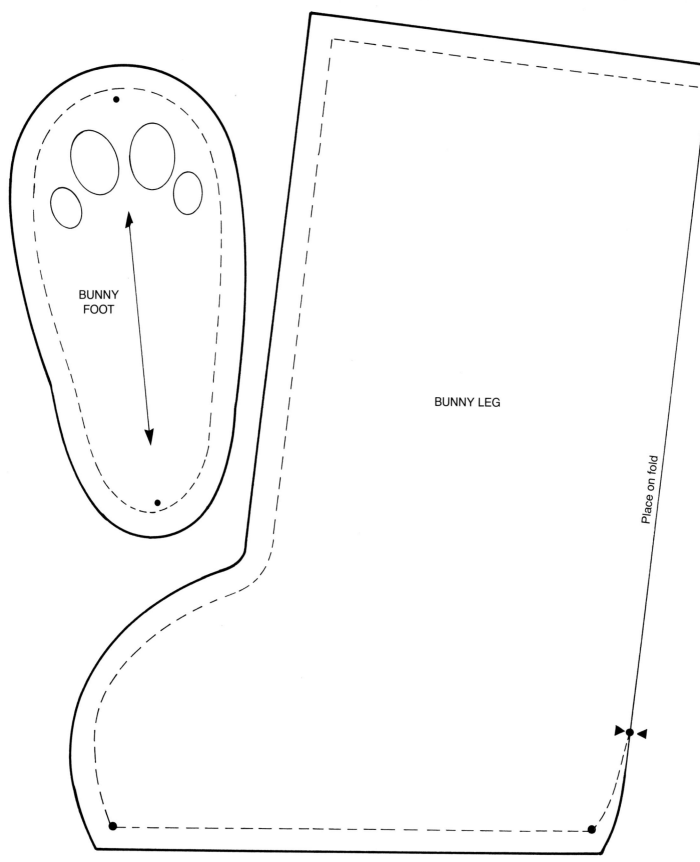

BUNNY FOOT

BUNNY LEG

Place on fold

EASTER PLANT STAKES

Girl Bunny Plant Stake

Making the Head

1. Trace the patterns on page 110. Cut two head fronts, one head back, and four of the girl's ears. Lightly trace the facial features onto the right side of each head front piece. Use permanent markers or use a water-soluble pen if you want to embroider the features later.

2. With right sides together, stitch two ear pieces together, leaving open at bottom. Trim and clip seam allowances; turn ear right side out. Make second ear in the same manner.

3. Hand-baste ears to right side of back head piece at markings, matching raw edges (Figure 1).

4. Position the head front pieces with right sides together. Stitch them together, beginning at the top of the head and stitching around the nose to the bottom of the neck; leave the back edges open.

5. Position front and back with right sides together, matching the center front seam to the center marking on the back. Stitch front head piece to back, securing the ears between the layers. Do not stitch below point A (Figure 2).

6. Trim and clip seam allowances. Turn head right side out. Stuff the nose area and the top of the head.

7. Apply glue to one end of the skewer and center it inside the head, poking it gently into the stuffing. Finish stuffing the head and neck around the skewer. Turn under the seam allowance at the side and hand-sew it closed.

8. Use heavy thread to tie the raw edges of the neck tightly around the skewer. Put a small amount of glue on the skewer under the neck to keep the head from turning on the skewer.

9. Complete the facial features with embroidery or permanent pens. Figure 3 is a front view of an embroidered face.

Making the Cape

1. Cut a 2½ × 11½-inch strip for the cape. Fold the strip in half lengthwise, right sides together, and stitch the two layers together ¼ inch from each short end. Turn the strip right side out and press.

2. Hand-sew a gathering thread ¼ inch from the raw edges.

3. Gather the cape tightly around the bunny's neck, positioning the ends of the strip at the back. Knot the gathering threads to secure the cape, but don't cut the thread. Use this thread to sew the cape neck to the bunny's neck.

4. Cut 3 inches of pregathered lace. Tack the lace over the raw edge of the neck band.

5. Cut 20-inch lengths of two ribbons. Wrap the ribbons around the

Approximate size:
4½ inches plus skewer

MATERIALS NEEDED:
Scraps of muslin and pink fabric
8 inches of ½-inch-wide
   pregathered lace
30 inches *each* of ⅛-inch-wide
   ribbons in at least two colors
Brown and pink embroidery
   floss for facial features
Small artificial flowers or
   ribbon roses
One 10-inch-long bamboo
   shish-kebab skewer
Crafts glue
Polyester filling

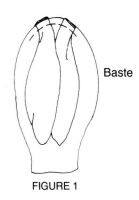

Baste

FIGURE 1

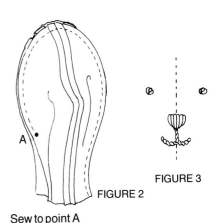

A

Sew to point A

FIGURE 2

FIGURE 3

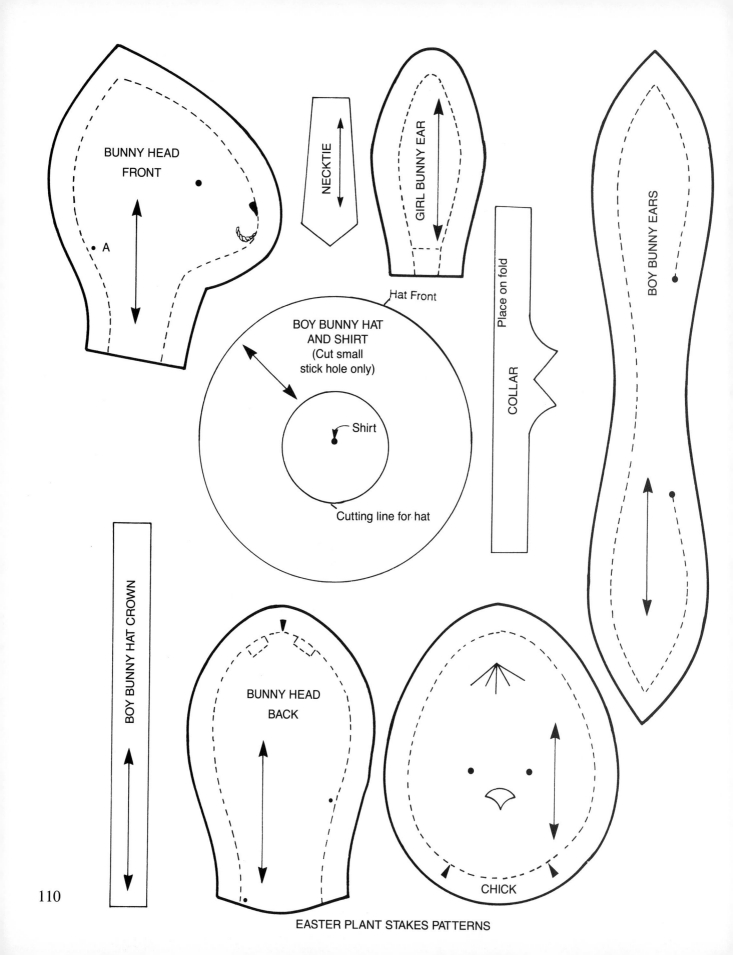

BUNNY HEAD
FRONT

A

NECKTIE

GIRL BUNNY EAR

BOY BUNNY EARS

Hat Front

Place on fold

BOY BUNNY HAT
AND SHIRT
(Cut small
stick hole only)

Shirt

COLLAR

Cutting line for hat

BOY BUNNY HAT CROWN

BUNNY HEAD
BACK

CHICK

110

EASTER PLANT STAKES PATTERNS

bunny's neck, covering the gathered edge of the lace. Tie ribbons tightly into a bow with long streamers. Cut ribbon streamers at various lengths.

Adding the Easter Bonnet and Trims

1. For the Easter bonnet, cut 4 inches of pregathered lace. Fit the lace around the bunny's ears and back of the head with the ruffled edge slanted toward the face. Tack lace into position.

2. Tack a 4-inch piece of ribbon in place to trim the top edge of the lace bonnet.

3. Tack or glue artificial flowers in front of the bunny's right ear.

4. Make a ribbon bow from at least four 4-inch lengths of ribbon; tack bow in place behind spray of flowers.

Boy Bunny Plant Stake

Making the Head

1. Follow the instructions for the Girl Bunny's head through Step 7, omitting the ears. The boy's ears are not sewn into the head seam.

2. Using the Boy Bunny's ear pattern, cut two ear pieces.

3. Stitch the ears with right sides together, leaving an opening in the center as shown on the pattern.

4. Trim and clip seam allowances. Turn ears right side out; slip-stitch the opening shut.

5. Tie a small knot in the center of the ears. Tack the knot to the top of the bunny's head, letting the ears droop (Figure 1).

Making the Shirt, Tie, and Collar

1. Cut one shirt piece. Clip a tiny opening in the center, as noted on the shirt pattern.

2. Hand-stitch a gathering thread around the shirt, ¼ inch from the outside edge. Pull up gathers loosely.

3. Referring to Figure 2, put skewer through the center opening of the

Approximate size:
3¼ inches plus skewer

MATERIALS NEEDED:
Scraps of blue and white fabric, muslin, and burlap
Scraps of stiff interfacing and paper-backed fusible webbing
1-inch-long piece of orange chenille stem
Brown, pink, and green embroidery floss
One 10-inch bamboo shish-kebab skewer
Crafts glue
Polyester filling

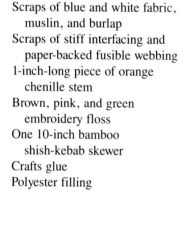

Knot ears
on top of head

FIGURE 1

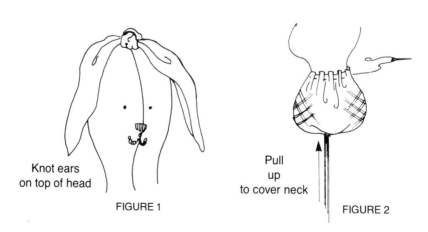

Pull
up
to cover neck

FIGURE 2

shirt; push the shirt up to the bottom of the head. Firmly stuff the shirt around the skewer. Pull the gathers tight around neck, then use the gathering thread to stitch the shirt to the neck.

4. Select a 2-inch-square fabric scrap for the tie. Fold the square in half and fuse the wrong sides together. Cut one of the tie pattern from the fused fabric. Tack the tie in place at the center front neck.

5. Cut a 2½ × 4-inch scrap of white fabric for the collar. Fold the fabric in half lengthwise and press. Place a 1 × 4-inch piece of fusible webbing *inside* the fold of the fabric and press. Peel off the remaining paper, fold the top layer of fabric down, and press again. Cut one of the collar pattern from this layered fabric on the fold as indicated. Tack the collar in place around bunny's neck.

Making the Hat

1. Make a stiff burlap sandwich by fusing stiff interfacing between two 4-inch squares of burlap. Cut one crown piece and one hat from this layered burlap. Cut the center opening in the hat to create the brim. (Note: The hole is off-center.)

2. Roll the crown piece to fit just inside the opening of the hat brim, extending above the brim (Figure 3). Hand-stitch the crown to the brim. Stitch crown closed in center back.

3. Cut a ⅝ × 4½-inch bias piece of shirt fabric to make the hat band. Fold both raw edges in until the band is ¼ inch wide (Figure 4). Tack band to brim of hat.

4. For the carrot, cut ten 1-inch pieces of green embroidery floss. Glue these short strands of floss to the top ⅜ inch of the chenille stem. Wrap more green floss around this top portion of the stem until no orange shows (Figure 5). Use glue to secure loose ends. Leave the remainder of the stem uncovered. Shape the floss carrot top with scissors; trim the bottom of the carrot into a point. Be careful not to cut the wire in the stem, as this may damage the scissors. Glue the carrot onto the hat brim.

5. Glue the hat onto the bunny's head.

FIGURE 3

Row edges folded inside

FIGURE 4

FIGURE 5

Chick Plant Stake

Approximate size:
4 inches plus skewer

MATERIALS NEEDED:
Scraps of muslin and three
  pastel print fabrics
24 inches *each* of ⅛-inch to ⅜-
  inch ribbons in three colors
Black and yellow embroidery
  floss for facial features
One 10-inch bamboo
  shish-kebab skewer
Crafts glue
Polyester filling

Making the Head

1. Cut two of the chick's head pattern. Trace the face onto the right side of one head piece. Use permanent pens to mark the facial features or use a water-soluble marker if you intend to embroider the features after completing the head.

2. Stitch head pieces with right sides together, leaving the bottom open as shown on the pattern. Trim and clip the seam allowances, then turn the head right side out. Stuff the top half of the head.

3. Put glue on one end of the skewer and center it inside head, poking it gently into the stuffing. Finish stuffing the head around the skewer. Turn under the seam allowance of the opening and sew it closed.

4. Put a little glue on the skewer under the head to keep the head from turning on the skewer.

Adding the Neck Bands and Ribbon Trim

1. Tear one 1 × 5-inch and two ¾ × 5-inch pieces of assorted pastel prints for neck bands. (Fringe is more attractive when fabrics are torn and have irregular edges than if they are cut.) Pull the fabric threads to fringe ¼ inch on one long side of the 1-inch neck band and one of the ¾-inch neck bands. Fringe both long sides of the remaining band.

2. With the widest strip on the bottom, layer the neck bands together right sides up. Stitch one gathering thread lengthwise through all layers, as shown in Figure 1.

3. Pull up gathers tightly to fit the bands around the chick's neck, overlapping the raw edges in back. Stitch neck bands in place. Use a dab of glue to secure the ends.

4. Cut 24-inch lengths of assorted ribbons. Loop the ribbons into bows with long streamers (Figure 2).

5. Tack bows in place; cut streamers to various lengths.

CHICK NECK BAND

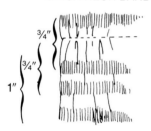

FIGURE 1

My Favorite Apron, Easter Style

The chick appliqué pattern, opposite, gives cheery flavor to my favorite apron. Use a pastel print fabric for the apron and solids for the appliqué. See Chapter 3 for patterns and instructions for the basic apron.

FIGURE 2

MY FAVORITE APRON—EASTER APPLIQUÉ PATTERN

Approximate size:
25 inches tall

MATERIALS NEEDED:
Scraps of assorted fabrics

CHAPTER NINE

INDEPENDENCE DAY

Red, White, and Blue A. Bear

For the Fourth of July, A. Bear is decked out in red, white, and blue. His sailor collar is made from the Thanksgiving bib pattern on page 148. The ties are made from a 4 × 45-inch strip that is stitched together lengthwise to make a tube, turned, pressed, and cut in half. Just sew the ties to the bib and tie it on backwards.

The Other Patriotic A. Bear
Don't forget the A. Bear on page 95, who looks like he is ready to step out in his "dress whites."

My Favorite Apron, Fourth of July Style

Only the appliqué design and base fabric are different for this version of my favorite apron. Use the heart pattern, opposite, for the appliqué; the patterns and instructions for the basic apron begin on page 27.

MY FAVORITE APRON—FOURTH OF JULY APPLIQUÉ PATTERN

A Scrappy Little Flag

This is a variation of the Tied Wreath in Chapter Three. While this book focuses on *fabric* scraps, it's fun to recycle other scraps, too. My mother's ability to find a second use for things, especially plastic containers and lids, is legend in our family. Creating this little project gave me a clue that her talent might be hereditary.

Make a "free" wreath form by cutting the center out of a plastic lid. I used a small one (from a can of potato chips), but the idea works on all sizes of plastic lids. Larger lids can be used to make small window wreaths.

To make the Scrappy Little Flag, cut a 1-inch-diameter hole in the center of a 3-inch-diameter plastic lid. Using bias strips about 10 inches long, tie navy blue star fabric in one quarter of the ring, then alternate red and white strips around the rest of the ring. Trim the strips to approximate a rectangular shape.

Star Wall Hanging

This wall hanging frames a simple Ohio Star block in patriotic stars and stripes.

Making the Ohio Star Block

1. You need 16 small triangles to make the four pieced units of this nine-patch block. Using the triangle pattern, below, cut four triangles of navy fabric, four triangles of ecru fabric, and eight triangles of red fabric. (If using striped fabric, position the pattern carefully when cutting.)

2. Referring to Figure 1, sew four triangles together to make a unit. Be sure to position the triangles to obtain correct color placement. Make four units in the same manner; each finished unit should measure 3¼ inches square. Press the seam allowances toward the red triangles.

3. Using the square pattern, cut five squares of ecru fabric. I used a fabric with a large star print for the center square.

4. Assemble the four pieced units and the five solid squares into rows, referring to Figure 2, then join the rows to complete the block.

Approximate size:
11 inches square

MATERIALS NEEDED:
Scraps of red, ecru, and navy fabrics
⅛ yard *each* of red and navy fabrics for the borders
⅜ yard of backing fabric
⅜ yard of quilt batting

FIGURE 1

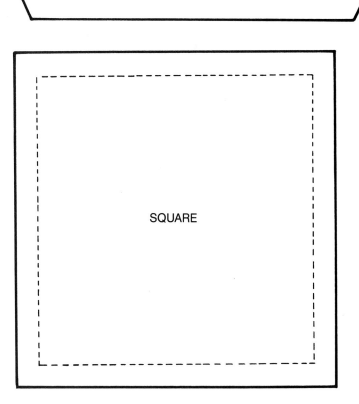

TRIANGLE

SQUARE

FIGURE 2

119

FIGURE 3

Adding the Border and Appliqué

Measure your block before cutting your border strips. The lengths given are mathematically correct, but your wall hanging may be slightly different.

1. For the inside border, cut two $\frac{7}{8} \times 9$-inch strips and two $\frac{7}{8} \times 9\frac{1}{2}$-inch strips.

2. Add the shorter strips to opposite sides of the block first, then add the longer strips to the remaining sides.

3. For the outside border, cut two $1\frac{5}{8} \times 9\frac{1}{2}$-inch strips and two $1\frac{5}{8} \times 11\frac{3}{4}$-inch strips. Add these in the same manner.

4. Using the heart pattern on page 87, cut four hearts. Position the hearts as shown in Figure 3. Appliqué each heart in place, using your favorite appliqué method as described in Chapter 2.

Finishing the Wall Hanging

This wall hanging is finished in a way slightly different from the traditional method. The quilt top is layered with a pieced backing and the batting, sewn together, and turned right side out through a seam in the backing.

1. From the remaining navy fabric, cut a right triangle with 9-inch legs. With right sides together, position the triangle at one corner of the backing fabric as shown in Figure 4. Machine-stitch approximately $2\frac{1}{2}$ inches in from each end of the diagonal side, leaving an opening as shown. Trim the backing fabric from the seam, leaving a $\frac{1}{4}$-inch seam allowance.

2. Layer batting, quilt top, and backing, with right sides of the top and backing together. Stitch a $\frac{1}{4}$-inch seam all around. Turn the quilt through the opening in the pieced backing. Slip-stitch the opening closed.

3. Quilt in the ditch of the seam lines of the borders and the block.

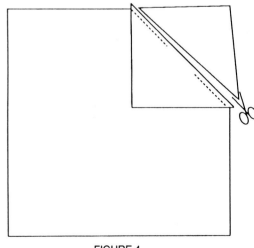

FIGURE 4

Approximate size:
25 inches tall

MATERIALS NEEDED:
4 × 20-inch scrap of felt for
  mask
½ yard *each* of two Halloween
  prints for cape and lining
Halloween fabric scraps to equal
  ¾ yard for bear's body
1⅝ yards of ¼-inch-wide black
  grosgrain ribbon
30 inches of ⅛-inch-wide
  orange satin ribbon

CHAPTER TEN

HALLOWEEN

Halloween A. Bear

Every part of this A. Bear's body is made from a different Halloween print fabric. Costumed in a dapper cape and mask, no one will ever guess his real identity on All Hallow's Eve. Turn to Chapter 4 for A. Bear's patterns and general construction techniques.

Making the Halloween Mask

1. Cut two mask pieces from felt.

2. Topstitch mask pieces together, stitching ¼ inch from all edges, including eye holes.

3. Hand-stitch a 13½-inch length of black ribbon to each side of the mask. Tie the mask over A. Bear's eyes and nose.

122

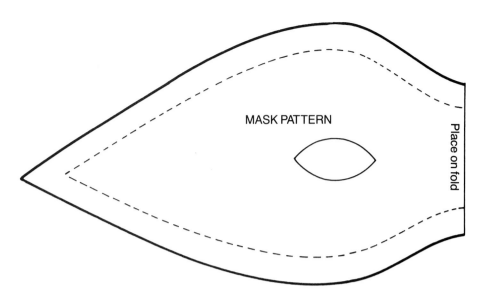

MASK PATTERN

Place on fold

Making the Halloween Cape

1. To make a pattern for the cape, draw a half-circle with a 14½-inch radius. Keeping the same center, draw another half-circle with a 3½-inch radius for the neck opening (Figure 1).

2. Using this pattern, cut two cape pieces from contrasting Halloween prints. (One piece will be the lining, which shows.)

3. With right sides together, stitch cape and lining pieces together. Leave a 3-inch opening at the bottom for turning.

4. Trim seam allowances; turn cape right side out. Slip-stitch the opening closed.

5. Use a long gathering stitch to sew two rows of gathers ¾ inch and 1 inch from the finished neck edge (Figure 2). Adjust gathers to fit the cape around the bear's neck, leaving a 2½-inch opening between the front edges.

6. Cut two 13½-inch lengths each of black ribbon and orange ribbon. On both sides of the cape, hand-sew one end of each color ribbon to the underside between the rows of gathering, ½ inch from the outside edge. Tie ribbons in a bow; trim ends as desired.

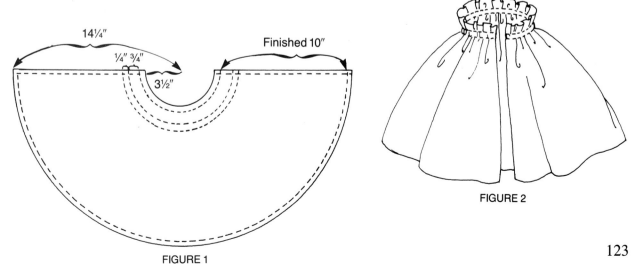

14¼″

¼″ 3¾″

3½″

Finished 10″

FIGURE 1

FIGURE 2

Witch and Scarecrow Rag Dolls

Approximate size:
7¼ inches tall

MATERIALS NEEDED:
Scraps of flesh-colored and
  denim fabrics
Polyester filling
Embroidery floss or permanent
  markers for facial features

Make these doll bodies following the directions for making the Christmas Rag Dolls (page 66), using the patterns for the angel head/body, arm, leg, and shoe. The witch has contrasting shoes; the scarecrow's legs and feet are cut in one piece from denim. The witch and scarecrow face patterns are opposite; the dotted line represents the *finished* size of the head. See the Halloween Witch Plant Stake (page 129) for instructions on adding the Witch's hair.

The Doll Clothes

Making the Witch's Dress

1. Cut one dress piece, placing the shoulder edge of the pattern on the fold of the fabric.

2. Slash the neck opening as shown in Figure 1. Turn facing to wrong side along fold lines and press to hold in place, if necessary. Hand-stitch facings down.

3. Trim sleeves to wrist length, using pinking shears, or cut jagged edges with scissors.

4. With right sides together, stitch underarm seams. At each side, pivot where the sleeve meets the skirt and stitch the skirt side seam. Clip corners, then turn dress right side out.

5. Put dress on doll. Trim skirt to let the witch's toes peek out from under the edge.

6. Make 1-inch- to 1½-inch-long slashes along the bottom of the skirt, spacing them ⅛ inch to ¼ inch apart.

MATERIALS NEEDED FOR WITCH:
¼ yard of assorted black fabric scraps
Scraps of heavy-weight interfacing
Paper-backed fusible webbing

MATERIALS NEEDED FOR SCARECROW:
Scraps of gingham, print, felt, denim, burlap
10 inches of jute twine
Scraps of polyester filling
Paper-backed fusible webbing

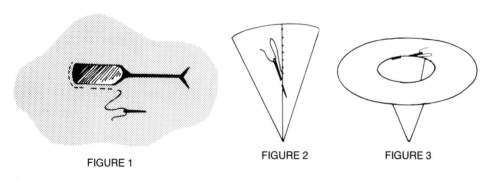

FIGURE 1   FIGURE 2   FIGURE 3

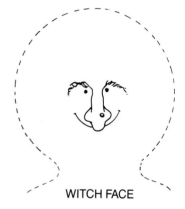

WITCH FACE

Making the Witch's Hat

1. Using paper-backed fusible webbing, make a stiff fabric sandwich by fusing interfacing between two 5 × 7-inch pieces of black fabric. From this layered fabric, cut one crown piece and one brim. Cut out the center opening of the brim as shown on the pattern.

2. Roll the crown piece into a cone to fit inside the opening in the brim. Fold under the exposed raw edge of the crown and slip-stitch the edge as shown in Figure 2.

3. Working on the wrong side of the brim, hand-stitch the crown to the inside opening of the brim (Figure 3).

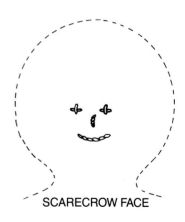

SCARECROW FACE

125

Making the Witch's Vest and Scarf

1. Cut one back vest piece on the fold and two front vest pieces.

2. Stitch fronts to back at shoulders.

3. Turn under the ¼-inch seam allowance around the neck and front edges of vest and topstitch.

4. Make 1-inch-long slashes around the bottom edge of the vest, varying the widths of the slashes.

5. For the scarf, cut a 1 × 14-inch piece of sheer black fabric. Tie the strip around the witch's neck, then slash the ends approximately 2 inches from the bottom.

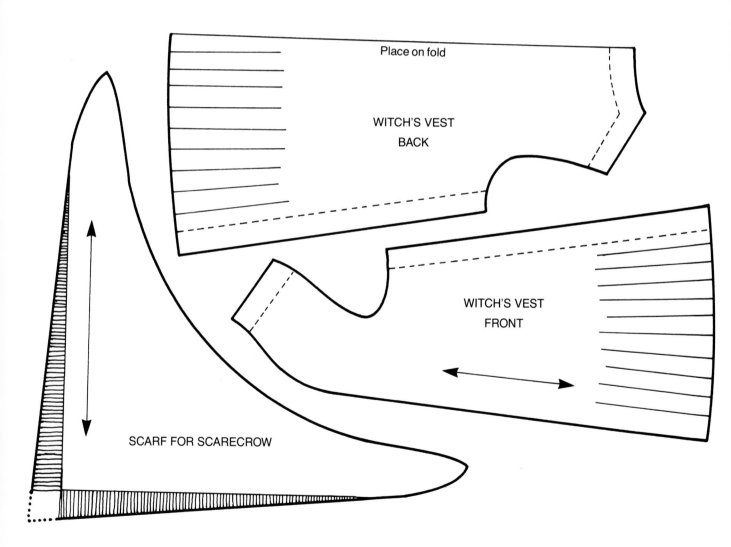

Place on fold

WITCH'S VEST
BACK

WITCH'S VEST
FRONT

SCARF FOR SCARECROW

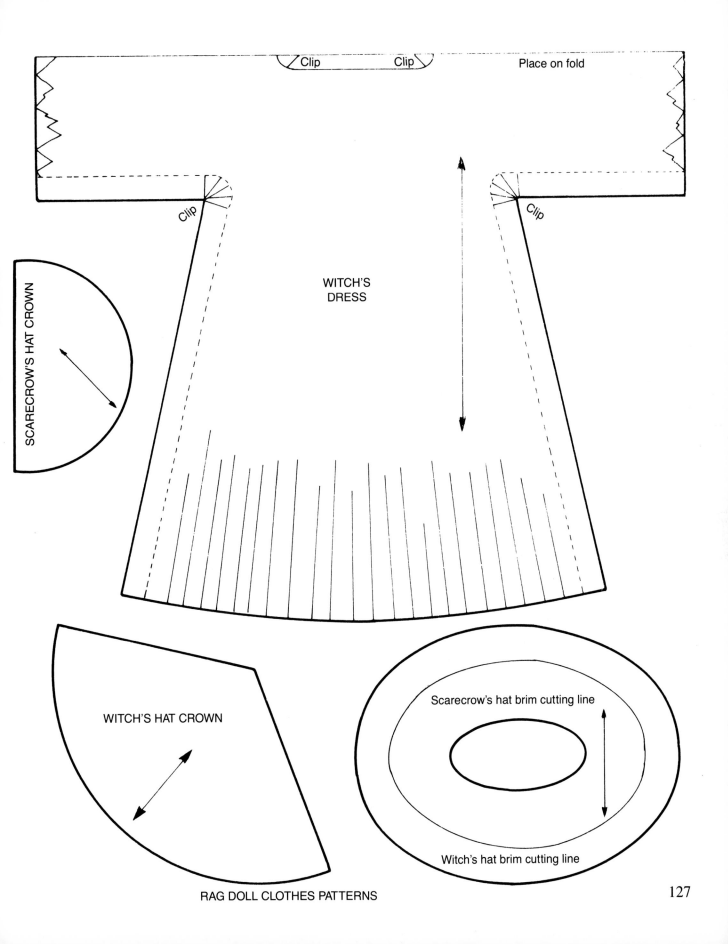

Clip   Clip   Place on fold

Clip   Clip

WITCH'S
DRESS

SCARECROW'S HAT CROWN

WITCH'S HAT CROWN

Scarecrow's hat brim cutting line

Witch's hat brim cutting line

RAG DOLL CLOTHES PATTERNS

127

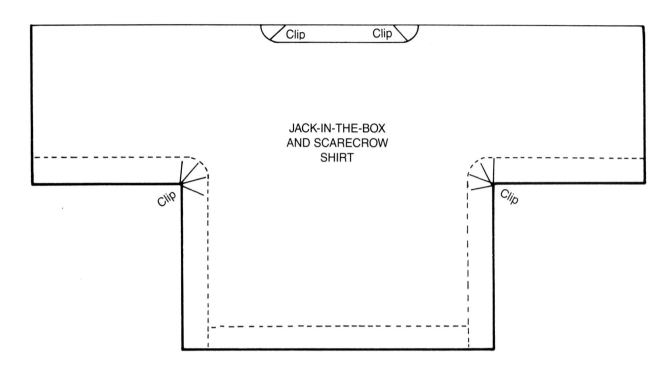

JACK-IN-THE-BOX
AND SCARECROW
SHIRT

Clip   Clip

Clip

Clip

Making the Scarecrow's Shirt

1. Cut one shirt piece on the fold.

2. Slash the neck opening as shown in Figure 1 for the witch's dress. Turn facing to the wrong side along fold lines; press to hold in place, if necessary, and hand-stitch facings down.

3. Press under ¼-inch hems on the sleeves and shirttail edges.

4. Cut one 2 × 12-inch piece of burlap. Fold the strip in half lengthwise and press.

5. Cut strips of the folded burlap to fit each wrist and the shirt front and back hems. Pin the folded edge of the burlap against the raw edge of the wrists and shirttails (Figure 4).

6. Stitch each burlap piece in place. Fringe the raw edges, then cut them in a jagged manner for a natural appearance.

7. With right sides of shirt together, stitch each underarm seam and pivot at the corner to stitch the side seam. Clip seam allowances at corners. Turn shirt right side out.

FIGURE 4

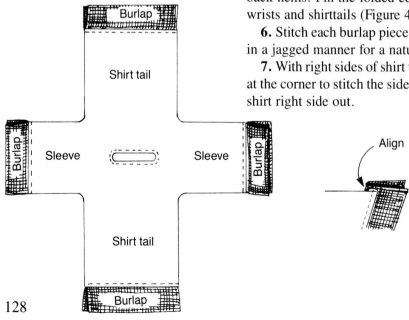

Burlap

Shirt tail

Burlap   Sleeve   Sleeve   Burlap

Shirt tail

Burlap

Align

Making the Scarecrow's Hat and Burlap Hair

1. Fuse two 2½ × 3½-inch pieces of felt with wrong sides together.

2. Cut one brim piece (page 127) from this layered fabric, cutting out the center opening as well.

3. Cut two crown pieces (page 127) from a single layer of felt. Whip the crown pieces together around the curved edge.

4. With the whipped edges of the crown on the outside, hand-sew the crown to the inside opening of the brim, using tiny stitches from the top side. Catch a few loose strands of burlap between the crown and brim as you sew them together.

5. Put the hat on the scarecrow to determine placement of loose burlap strands for the hair. Remove the hat, then tack burlap strands to the underside of the hat.

Scarecrow's Scarf and Accessories

1. Cut one fabric scarf piece exactly as illustrated on pattern (page 126). With the grainline as marked, the cut edges will be off-grain and will ravel unevenly, as shown. Tie the scarf around the scarecrow's neck. Adjust as desired and tack in place.

2. Tack scraps of fringed fabric onto the legs for patches.

3. Put a small wad of stuffing inside the shirt to fill out the scarecrow's belly. Tie twine around the scarecrow's waist for a belt.

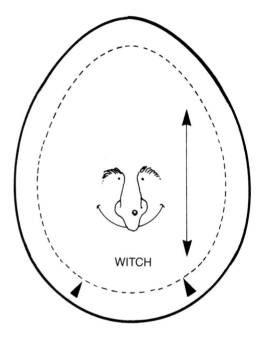

WITCH

HALLOWEEN PLANT STAKES

Witch Plant Stake

Making the Head

Using the head pattern, right, follow instructions for the Easter Chick's head (page 114) to make the witch's head. Draw the facial features with permanent ink pens, adding a dab of textile paint for the beguiling wart.

Making the Cape

1. Cut one black cape piece. Cut out the circular opening in the center as indicated on the cape pattern.

2. Run a gathering thread around the neck opening ¼ inch from the edge.

3. Slide the cape into position on the skewer under the head; gather the neck edge tightly around the skewer. Wrap the thread around the gathers; knot the thread. Dab glue on the skewer under the neck to prevent the cape from sliding down.

4. Cut two shoulder pieces from heavy interfacing.

5. Slide shoulder pieces up under cape to create a shoulder line. Apply a dab of glue between layers of interfacing and between the cape and the interfacing to hold the shoulders in place.

Approximate size:
6½ inches (including hat), plus skewer

MATERIALS NEEDED:
Scraps of muslin and black cotton fabric
Curly crepe-wool hair
Scraps of heavy interfacing
Paper-backed fusible webbing
10 inches *each* of narrow orange and green ribbons
Polyester filling
One 10-inch bamboo shish-kebab skewer
Permanent markers, textile paint for facial features

6. Tear a 1×5-inch piece of cape fabric for the neck band. (Fringe is more attractive if fabrics are torn and have irregular edges than if they are cut.) Pull the fabric threads to fringe ¼ inch on each long side of the strip.

7. Stitch a gathering thread lengthwise down the center of the band; pull gathers to fit the band around the neck (Figure 1). Sew or glue band in place.

8. Tie orange and green ribbons in a knot around the neck, letting the ribbon ends hang loose.

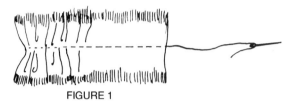

FIGURE 1

Making the Witch's Hair

1. Cut a 2-inch-long strand of curly crepe-wool hair. Separate the strand into four bunches.

2. Space the bunches evenly around the back of the head, 1 inch above the neck line (Figure 2). Sew or glue hair in place.

3. Cut a 3½-inch-long strand of crepe-wool hair. Separate this strand into four bunches. Sew or glue these bunches in place on the back of the head 2 inches above the neck line (Figure 3).

4. Position longer strands to go over the top of the head and down to the eyes to make bangs. (The hat will cover the crown of the head.) Separate the strands of hair; fluff and shape as desired.

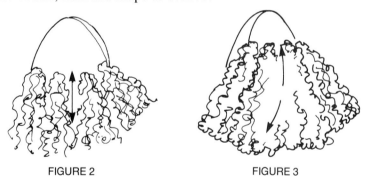

FIGURE 2   FIGURE 3

Making the Witch's Hat

1. Using fusible webbing, make a stiff fabric sandwich by fusing stiff interfacing between two 5×9-inch pieces of black fabric.

2. From this layered fabric, cut one crown and one brim. Cut the center opening in the brim.

3. Roll the crown piece into a cone to fit around the opening in the brim (¼-inch margin will extend all around). Fold under the raw edge of the crown and slip-stitch the edge. Hand-stitch the crown to the brim (Figure 4).

4. Glue the hat on the witch's head. It may be necessary to adjust the size of the brim opening to fit.

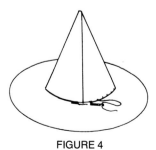

FIGURE 4

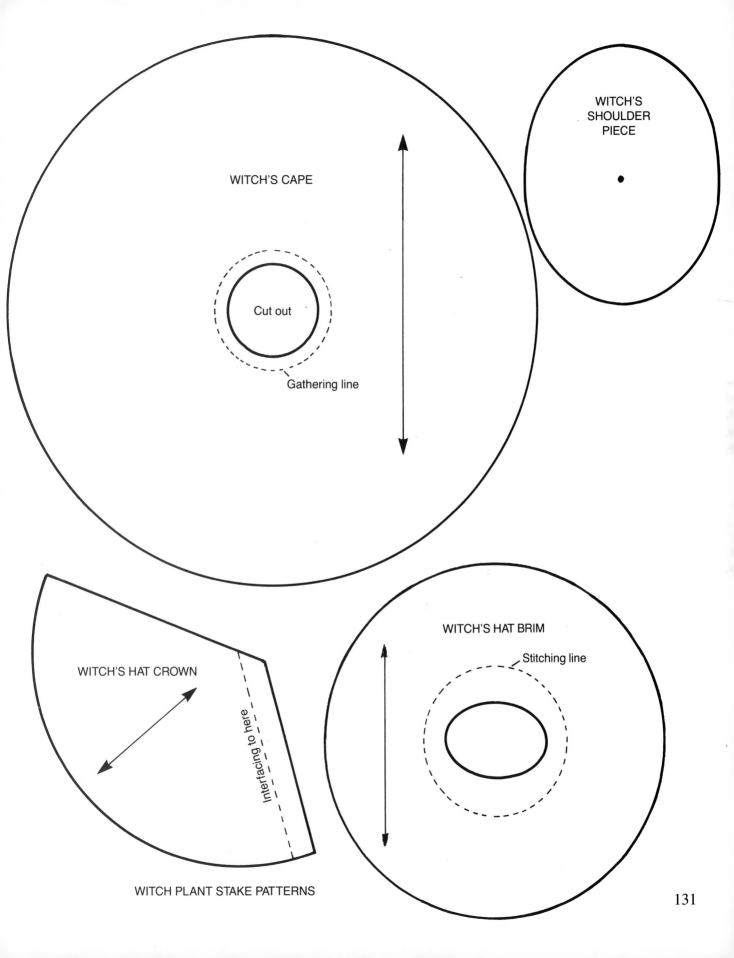

WITCH'S CAPE

WITCH'S SHOULDER PIECE

Cut out

Gathering line

WITCH'S HAT BRIM

Stitching line

WITCH'S HAT CROWN

Interfacing to here

WITCH PLANT STAKE PATTERNS

Pumpkin Plant Stake

Approximate size:

3½ inches plus skewer

MATERIALS NEEDED:

One 2½-inch-diameter plastic
    foam ball

Scraps of orange, green, and
    black fabrics

10 inches of heavy string

96 inches of orange embroidery
    floss or fine yarn

Plastic knife

Spanish moss, raffia, or
    excelsior

48-inch lengths of assorted
    ⅛-inch-wide ribbons

One 10-inch-long bamboo
    shish-kebab skewer

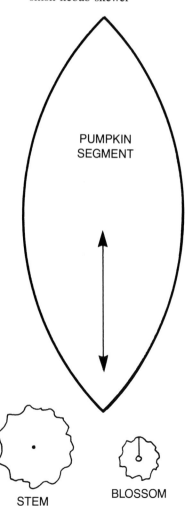

PUMPKIN
SEGMENT

STEM

BLOSSOM

1. Wind the string around the foam ball and pull it tightly to define eight equal wedge-shaped sections. Begin by dividing the ball into halves, then quarters and eighths. Pull the string tight enough to make an indentation approximately ⅛ inch deep. You may need to use a knife to make the indentations deep enough (Figure 1).

2. Using the segment pattern, cut eight pieces of orange fabric.

3. Lay each wedge-shaped piece of fabric over one section of the foam ball, then use the plastic knife to work the raw edges of fabric into the indentations. Smooth the fabric as you work. If necessary, use glue to secure the tips of each fabric piece.

4. Cut four pieces of embroidery floss, each 20–24 inches long. Wind the floss at least twice around the ball, forcing it into one indentation to cover the raw edges of the fabric (Figure 2). Tie the floss tightly into a knot at the bottom of the pumpkin. Fill each indentation in this manner.

5. Put a dab of glue on the end of the skewer, then push the skewer up into the bottom of the pumpkin. It may be necessary to clip the fabric, but be careful not to clip the embroidery floss holding the fabric in place.

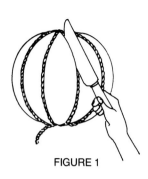

FIGURE 1

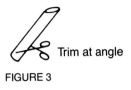

Floss

FIGURE 2

Trim at angle

FIGURE 3

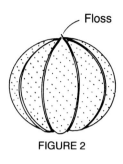

Face

6. Cut blossom and stem sections (these are the botanically correct names for the bottom and top) from green fabric. Glue the blossom at the bottom of the pumpkin, around the skewer, covering the knots of the floss. Glue the stem to the top of the pumpkin.

7. From the same green fabric, cut a 1⅛ × 2-inch strip. Apply glue to the wrong side of this fabric, then roll it along the narrow side to make a stem 1⅛ inches long. Let the glue dry.

8. Trim each end of the stem at parallel 45-degree angles (Figure 3). Glue stem atop the pumpkin stem piece.

9. Cut eyes, nose, and mouth pieces from black fabric; glue these into position on the pumpkin.

Adding the Wreath

Place Spanish moss on wax paper. Shape it into an open, airy wreath approximately 2 inches in diameter. Dribble glue onto the wreath to secure the shape; let glue dry. Weave ribbons through the wreath, using tiny drops of glue to hold them in place. Glue wreath in position at the bottom of the pumpkin. Make a bow from the remaining ribbons, and glue it in place on the wreath.

Halloween Wall Hanging

Making the Quilt Top

1. From the solid black fabric, cut a 9½-inch square and two 5-inch squares. From the Halloween print fabrics, cut 10 more 5-inch squares. I found a darling printed pumpkin fabric, but I've included a pumpkin appliqué pattern if you need to appliqué it onto a dark background. On this particular fabric, the ghosts that cavort around the printed pumpkins *glow in the dark*—which I did not realize until I walked through a darkened room where the quilt was hanging. Surprise!

2. Back scraps of white and black fabrics for appliqué with fusible webbing. Cut and position all appliqués needed. Fuse appliqués in place on background squares.

Approximate size:
25 inches square

MATERIALS NEEDED:
½ yard of black solid fabric
Three print or solid fabrics in Halloween colors
Scraps of white fabric for ghosts
⅛ yard of purple solid fabric for inside border
¼ yard of Halloween print fabric for outside border
18-inch square of organza
¾ yard *each* of paper-backed fusible webbing, batting, and backing fabric
Silver fabric paint with fine dispensing nozzle
Artificial spiders (or pom-poms and pipe cleaners)

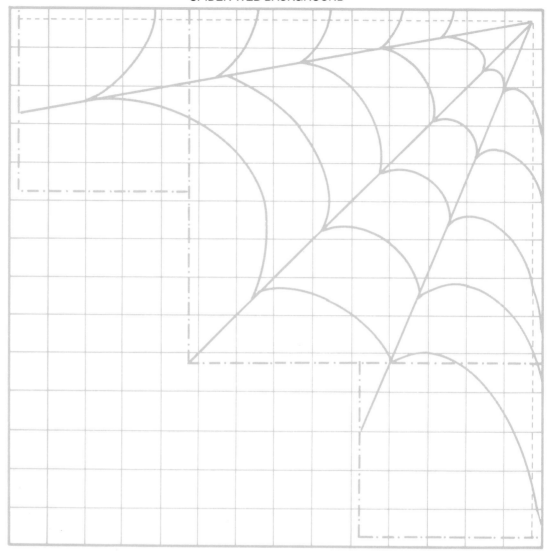

Scale: 1 square = 1 inch

FIGURE 1

3. Assemble the background squares in sets of four (Figure 1), then sew the four quarters together.

4. Enlarge the pattern for the spider web background, then trace it onto paper-backed fusible webbing. Cut out the web and fuse it to organza. Trim the excess organza and fuse the web in place on the black corner of the quilt. Mark the web spokes.

Adding the Borders

1. For the inner border, cut four $1\frac{1}{2} \times 20$-inch strips of purple fabric and four $1\frac{1}{2}$-inch orange squares.

2. Sew border strips to the side edges of the quilt top. Trim the ends of the strips even with the patchwork.

HALLOWEEN WALL HANGING
APPLIQUÉ PATTERNS

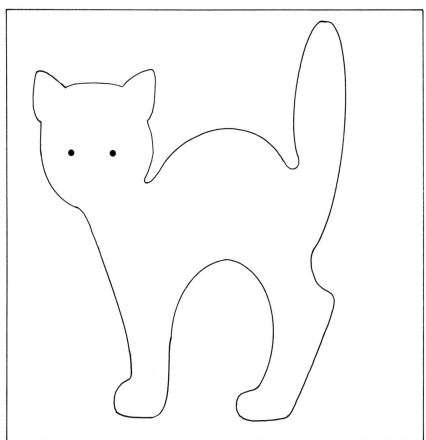

3. Stitch a square to one end of each remaining border strip. Carefully measure the exact length of the border needed, comparing the strips with the remaining sides of the wall hanging; trim strips as necessary, then sew orange squares to the other end of each strip. Stitch borders to top and bottom edges of the quilt top.

4. For the outer border, cut four 3¼ × 21-inch strips of Halloween print fabric and four 3¼-inch squares of a contrasting fabric. Add borders and squares in the same manner as for the inner border.

Finishing the Wall Hanging

1. Follow the instructions for the Irish Chain Wall Hanging (page 96) for preparing the backing fabric, layering, stitching, and turning the top through the pieced backing.

2. Machine-quilt on the marked spider web spokes and in the ditch of the seams around the other squares and the borders.

3. Add zigzag stitch detailing, embroidery, or sequin eyes as desired. Zigzag satin-stitch around the appliqués is optional.

4. Stitch ¼ inch from the edge of the quilt to give the illusion of a separate binding.

5. Practice using the fabric paint on a scrap, following the manufacturer's directions. Then paint the spider web spokes. Let paint dry completely before tacking or gluing the spider in place.

Haunted House

While the Haunted House was originally designed to be a seasonal tissue box cover and does have a chimney for dispensing tissue, it can also be used as a centerpiece, or filled with weighted boxes and used as a doorstop.

Making the House Walls

1. Enlarge the pattern for the house from the grid on page 141. Cut two house pieces each from the fabric, batting, and lining.

2. Cut the appliqués from the appropriate fabrics, using the patterns on page 144. The detail pieces that are not duplicated in full-size must be copied from the enlarged house pattern.

3. With right sides together, join the two house sections at the single-notched edge (Figure 1).

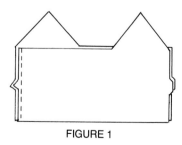

FIGURE 1

Approximate size:
4 × 10 × 12 inches

MATERIALS NEEDED:
⅜ yard of fabric for house
⅜ yard of lining fabric
Fabric scraps for chimney and appliqués
Batting
Fusible webbing
Fabric paints (optional)
Two standard-size tissue boxes (optional)

FIGURE 2

4. Some of the smaller design units are fused to each other before they are fused onto the house. For example, bats are fused onto round windows and one ghost is fused onto a long window. We cut holes in the fabric of the dirty windows to represent broken glass and then fused them to solid black fabric the size of the window. Experiment with the scraps you have available until you are satisfied with the results, then fuse the appliqués to the house in a logical order or, if necessary, let a pleasing arrangement overrule. Shutters really can't be *behind* the windows as on the house photographed, but I found the result more pleasing than when the shutters fell in front of the windows (Figure 2).

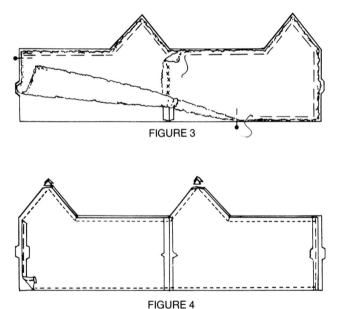

FIGURE 3

FIGURE 4

5. Lap the single-notched edges of the two batting pieces over each other as shown in Figure 3 and lightly catch-stitch them together. Baste the batting to the wrong side of the house, matching raw edges.

6. Stitch the lining pieces together at the single-notched edge. Press under the ¼-inch seam allowance on each double-notched edge of the lining and baste.

7. Pin the lining to the house with right sides together. Stitch along upper and lower edges only (Figure 4). Cut the roof top corners diagonally; clip seam allowances at corners.

HAUNTED HOUSE PATTERNS

Scale: 1 square = 1 inch

FIGURE 5

8. Turn the house right side out through one side. Topstitch through all layers at each of the house corners (Figure 5). Finish edges of appliqué if desired with satin-stitch or fabric paint. Add trim lines to the front windows and the windows over the door. Add vine to back of house with fabric paint.

9. Stitch the ends of the house together, keeping the lining free. Finger-press the seam allowances open. Push the seam allowances underneath the lining. Slip-stitch lining edges together.

Making the Roof

1. Cut roof, lining, and batting pieces, each $10 \times 11\frac{3}{8}$ inches.

2. Baste the batting to the wrong side of the roof fabric, matching all raw edges.

3. Stitch the lining to the roof, right sides together, leaving an opening for turning. Cut the corners diagonally, then turn the roof right side out.

4. Referring to the roof diagram opposite, topstitch the center (peak) line through all layers to create a fold line. Machine-quilt the roof parallel to the peak to create texture for the shingles. The illustrations opposite show two possible designs for shingles. Pick one or use your own, but remember to work each half of the roof with the shingles pointing up.

5. Fuse the spook appliqué to the roof.

Making the Chimney

1. Using the chimney pattern, page 144, cut one of fabric and one of batting. Baste the batting to the wrong side of the chimney fabric, matching raw edges.

2. Fold the chimney in half with wrong sides together. Stitch the angular, or uneven, edge of the chimney together (Figure 6). Clip seam allowances as necessary, then turn the chimney right side out. At this point, the top and bottom edges of the chimney are finished.

3. Fold the chimney to match raw edges (Figure 7) and machine-stitch them together. Clip the batting out of the seam allowance. Turn the raw edges to the inside and whip them down to hide the seam allowance at the chimney top.

4. Position the chimney on the roof, surrounding the designated hole. Position the shorter side of the chimney toward the peak of the roof. Slip-stitch the chimney in place on the roof.

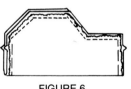

FIGURE 6

FIGURE 7

142

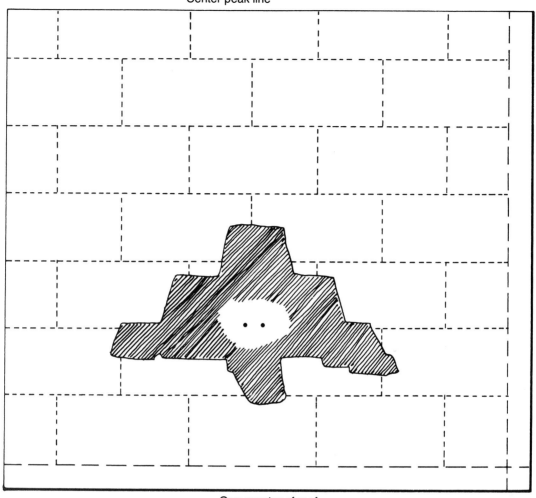

One-quarter of roof

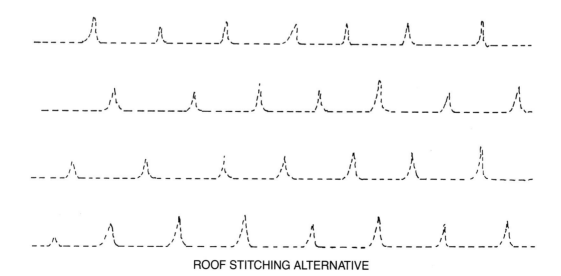

ROOF STITCHING ALTERNATIVE

143

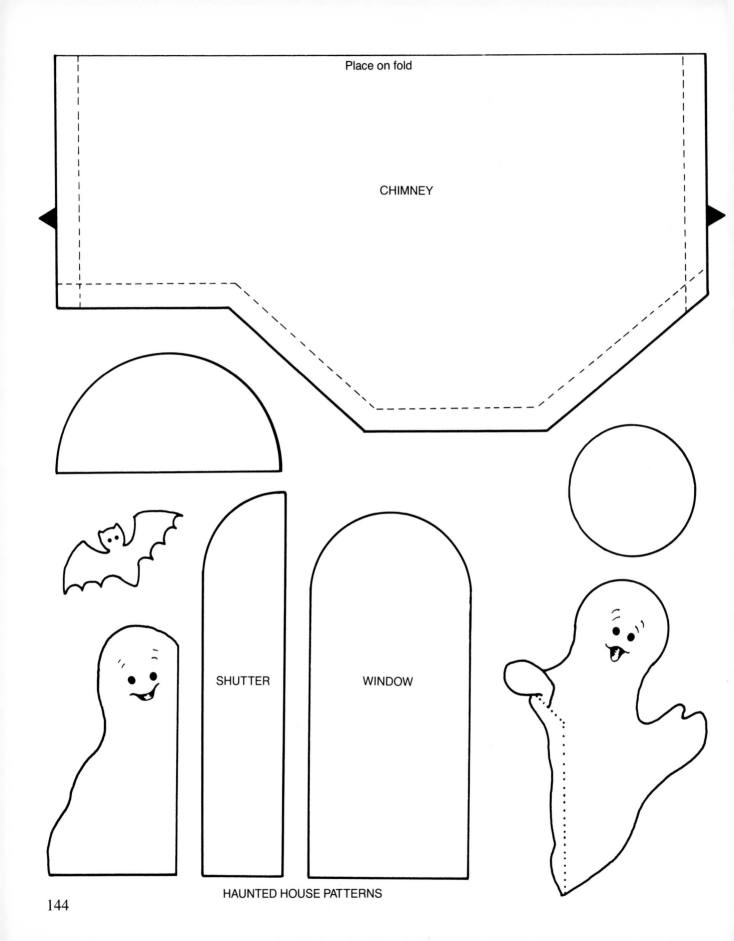

Place on fold

CHIMNEY

SHUTTER

WINDOW

HAUNTED HOUSE PATTERNS

144

Finishing the House

1. If you want to dispense tissue through the chimney, make a hole in the roof before attaching the chimney. Draw a square on the roof as indicated in Figure 8. Stitch around this square just *outside* the cutting line; stitch again ¼ inch away. Cut out the opening and clip the corners as shown.

2. Pin the roof to the house, right side out, positioning the chimney on the back side of the house (Figure 9). Align the gables of the house with the roof peak. The roof edges will extend ¾ inch beyond the upper edges of the house. Slip-stitch the roof to the house from the inside.

Haunted House Sweatshirt

If a spooky sweatshirt is your style, the Haunted House pattern can be adjusted so that it can be appliquéd onto a shirt front.

1. Cut the front side of the Haunted House from base fabric, excluding the gabled end and seam allowances. Cut a 9½ × 11-inch trapezoid for the roof.

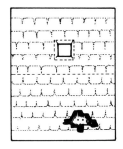

FIGURE 8

FIGURE 9

Approximate size:
25 inches tall

MATERIALS NEEDED:
⅞ yard of fabric for A. Bear
    body
¼ yard of white fabric
1 yard of 2-inch-wide black
    ribbon or fabric for tie
Polyester filling
Purchased eyes and nose
    (optional)

CHAPTER ELEVEN

THANKSGIVING

Thanksgiving A. Bear with Pilgrim Collar

1. Follow the directions in Chapter 4 to make A. Bear.

2. The collar is made and lined with the same white fabric, therefore it is necessary to cut four fronts and two backs. Interfacing is optional.

3. With right sides together, sew two front pieces to one back piece. Make the lining in the same manner as the collar, but leave one shoulder seam open between dots.

4. With right sides together, stitch collar to lining.

5. Trim and clip seam allowances. Turn collar right side out through shoulder seam opening. Slip-stitch the opening closed.

6. Tack collar in place around A. Bear's neck. Add ribbon tie.

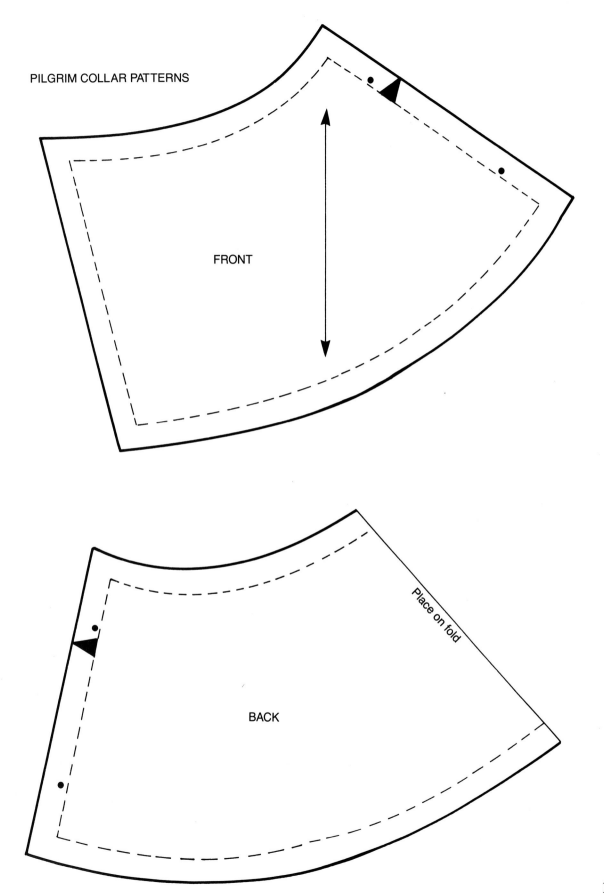

PILGRIM COLLAR PATTERNS

FRONT

BACK

Place on fold

147

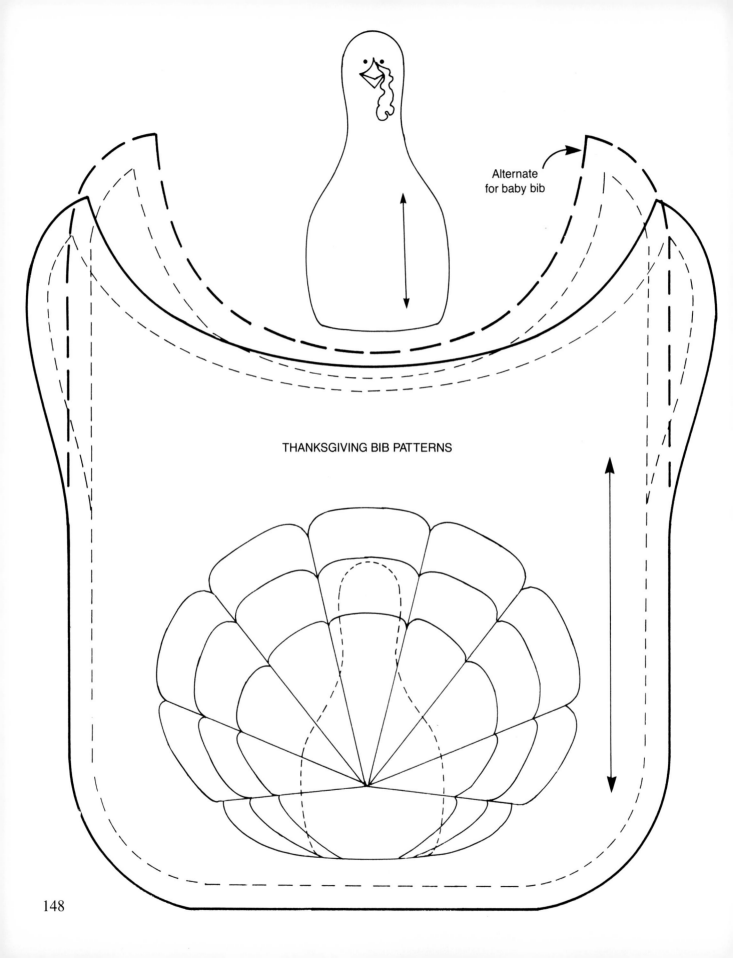

Alternate
for baby bib

THANKSGIVING BIB PATTERNS

148

A. Bear's Thanksgiving Bib

Turn to page 95 to see A. Bear sporting this Thanksgiving finery.

1. Cut two of the bib pattern from print fabric for the bib front and back. Cut one of the bib pattern from interfacing.

2. Fuse interfacing to the wrong side of the bib back.

3. Stitch front and back together, leaving 2 inches open on one side. Trim seam allowances; clip curves. Turn right side out and close the opening.

4. Trace the turkey's body and tail pieces onto the paper backing of the fusible webbing. Rough-cut the fusible pieces; fuse them to assorted print fabrics, then cut the fused fabric on the traced lines. Fuse each piece in place on the bib front.

5. Trace feather detail lines onto the tail. Machine-stitch a narrow row of zigzag stitching along detail lines, the outside edge of the tail, and around the turkey's body.

6. Fuse two small scraps of yellow fabric wrong sides together. Cut a beak from this fused fabric. Embroider the beak opening with brown floss. Secure a 2-inch-long piece of red embroidery floss to the back of the beak to make the wattle, then fuse or stitch the beak in place on the turkey's head. Embroider or paint the eyes.

7. Hand-stitch two 11-inch lengths of ribbon to each side of the bib for neck ties. Tie bib in place around A. Bear's neck.

Baby's First Thanksgiving Bib

To make a holiday bib for a baby's first Thanksgiving, use the alternate neckline on the bib pattern and complete as for A. Bear's bib.

Turkey Centerpiece

Finally, a turkey that survives Thanksgiving and returns again next year. This cute turkey can be used as a centerpiece or attached to a wreath for a door decoration.

Making the Turkey Body

1. Cut two body pieces and one base/back piece from turkey fabrics. Cut one base/back piece from heavy interfacing without seam allowances.

2. Stitch a gathering thread ⅛ inch from the edge around the base/back fabric. Fuse the interfacing inside the seam allowance of the base/back. Gather fabric edge to inside of base/back (Figure 1).

3. Stitch the body pieces together, leaving the base and back open. Stitch a gathering thread ⅛ inch from the bottom edge. Clip the seam allowances, then turn the body right side out. Stuff the neck and body very firmly.

4. Turn under the ¼-inch seam allowances on the unsewn edges of the body. Matching the front and back dots of the base/back to the seams of the

Approximate size:
7½ inches square

MATERIALS NEEDED:
Scraps of assorted holiday print
    fabrics and coordinating solid
    fabrics
Heavy interfacing
Brown and red embroidery floss
Fabric paint
Paper-backed fusible webbing
22 inches *each* of ¼-inch-wide
    brown and tan ribbons

Approximate size:
10 inches high

MATERIALS NEEDED:
Scrap fabrics for body and
    fantail back
Scraps of cotton print fabrics or
    burlap for ruffles
Cardboard and appropriate
    cutting tools
Polyester filling
Scraps of heavy interfacing,
    fusible webbing, and fleece
Hot-glue gun
Beads or floss for eyes

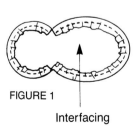

FIGURE 1

Interfacing

FIGURE 2

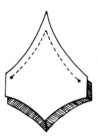

FIGURE 3

body, slip-stitch base/back to body. Gather body and base/back to fit as necessary (Figure 2).

5. Add beads or large French knots for eyes.

Making the Beak and Wattle

1. Cut two upper beak pieces and one lower beak piece. Stitch upper beaks together at top center seam. Stitch lower beak to lower edges of upper beak (Figure 3). Clip seam allowances and turn beak right side out. Stuff beak very firmly.

2. Turn under raw edges of beak. Slip-stitch it in place on the turkey's head, adding more stuffing as necessary.

3. Cut two wattle pieces. Sew them together, leaving the small end open. Clip seam allowances; turn the wattle right side out. Press.

4. Run a knotted thread up through the center of the tube, pulling it to gather the wattle for a crinkled look (Figure 4). Secure thread.

5. Turn the seam allowance at the open end of the wattle to the inside. Stitch the wattle to the top of the beak, letting it flop over to one side.

FIGURE 4

Making the Fantail Back

1. Apply fusible webbing to fleece, then cut one of the fantail pattern on page 154. From the fabric for the fantail back, rough-cut two fantail pieces.

2. Fuse the fleece to the wrong side of one fantail fabric piece.

3. Position the tail pieces with right sides together. With the fleece side faceup, stitch them together just outside the edge of the fleece. Leave an opening for turning.

4. Clip the seam allowances, then turn the tail right side out and press. Stitch the opening closed by hand.

5. Stitching through all layers, machine-quilt the feather detail lines as shown on the fantail pattern.

Cutting the Cardboard Rings

Cut cardboard rings, using the patterns on page 155. The patterns are shown as half-circles in order to fit on the page. Cut your rings as complete circles. If at least one piece of cardboard is heavy, the others can be a lighter weight. The edges of the rings do not have to be very smooth, as they will be camouflaged by the fabric ruffles.

Make one cut through each ring as indicated on the patterns, slightly rounding the corners of each cut.

The ruffles that cover these rings can be made from cotton-type fabrics or burlap. Use the following instructions for the fabric type that most closely resembles your fabric.

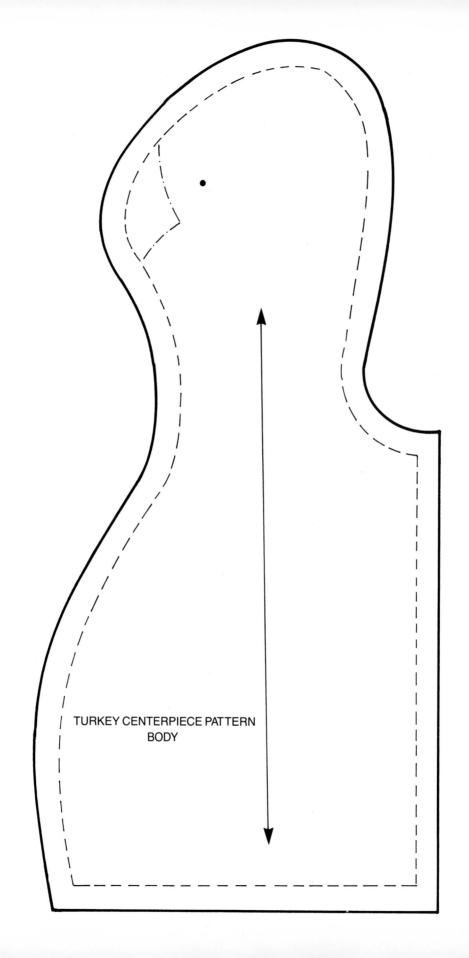

TURKEY CENTERPIECE PATTERN
BODY

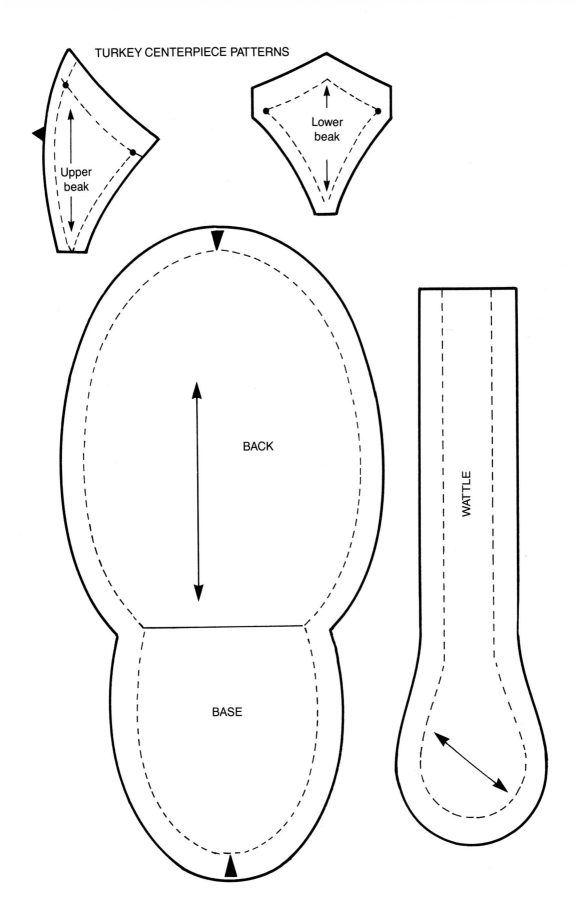

TURKEY CENTERPIECE PATTERNS

Upper beak

Lower beak

BACK

BASE

WATTLE

153

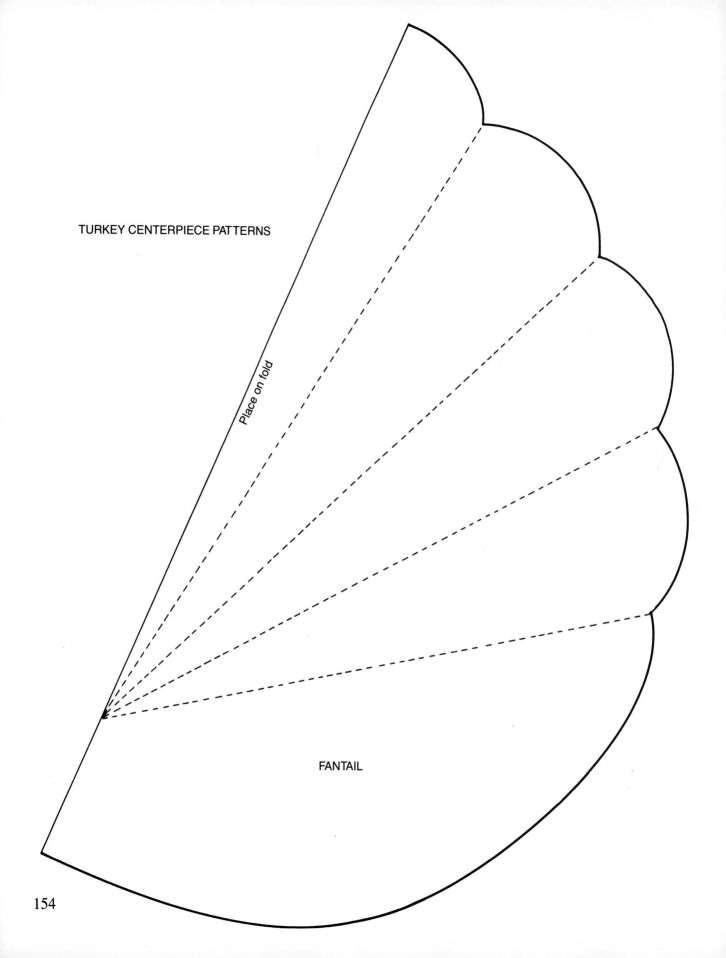

TURKEY CENTERPIECE PATTERNS

Place on fold

FANTAIL

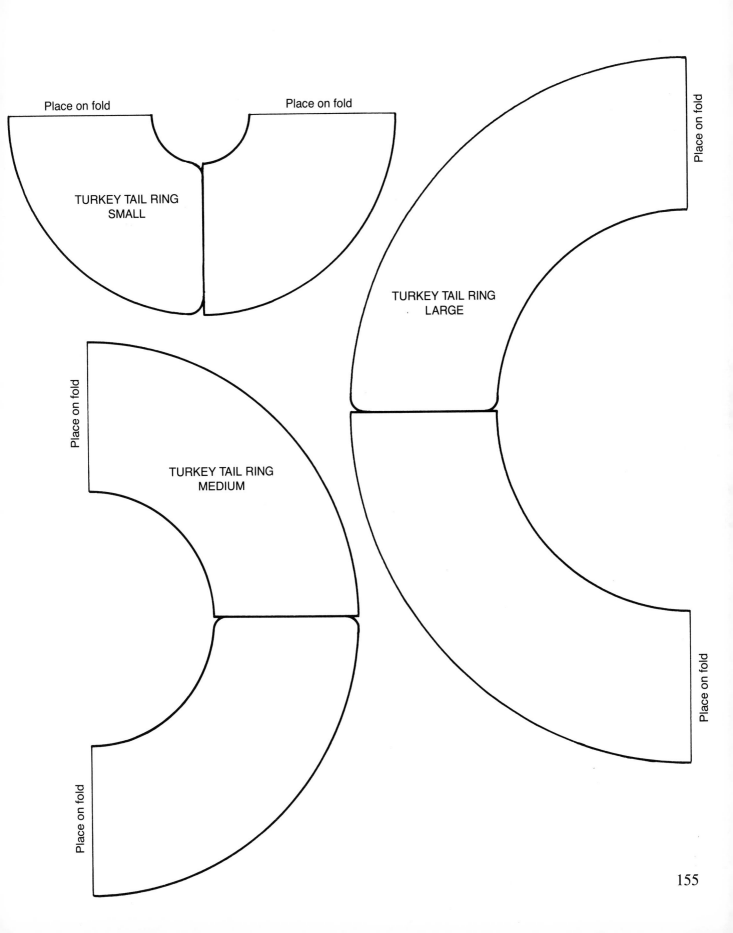

Place on fold

Place on fold

TURKEY TAIL RING
SMALL

Place on fold

TURKEY TAIL RING
LARGE

Place on fold

TURKEY TAIL RING
MEDIUM

Place on fold

Place on fold

Making Fabric Ruffles

Note: Extremely lightweight fabrics may be cut slightly longer than the lengths given, up to three times the circumference of the ring.

1. Cut one 7 × 30-inch fabric strip. Stitch the long raw edges right sides together. Turn the tube side out and press, positioning the seam approximately 1 inch from one fold.

2. Machine-stitch 1⅞ inches from the same folded edge, making a casing for the cardboard ring (Figure 5). This will enclose the seam allowance in the casing.

3. Thread the tube onto the 4-inch-diameter ring. Gather the fabric evenly around the ring. At the bottom opening, fold the ruffle behind the ring and glue the edges in place (Figure 6).

4. Complete the additional rings in the same manner. To cover the 5½-inch-diameter ring, cut a 7 × 45-inch fabric strip; for the 7-inch-diameter ring, work with a 7 × 67-inch strip.

5. Layer the ruffled rings from smallest to largest with the seamed sides toward the back and bottom edges even. Glue the layers together, then glue them atop the fantail back.

6. Sew or glue the body on top of the ruffled feather rings.

Making Burlap Ruffles

1. Cut a 6¼ × 20-inch strip of burlap. Fringe 1 inch of fabric on one long edge and ¾ inch on the other. Fold the strip lengthwise slightly off center; stitch 2¼ inches from the folded edge to make a casing for the cardboard ring (Figure 7).

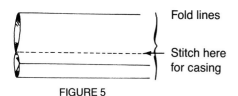

Fold lines

Stitch here for casing

FIGURE 5

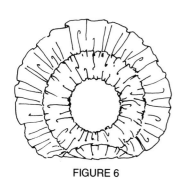

FIGURE 6

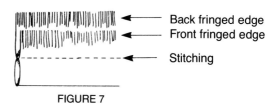

Back fringed edge
Front fringed edge
Stitching

FIGURE 7

2. Thread the tube onto the 4-inch cardboard ring and gather it evenly. Burlap is much stiffer to thread onto the ring than fabric, and the gathering may resemble pleats. When the cardboard ring is as full as possible, fold the ruffle at the bottom edge up onto the back of the cardboard ring and glue it in place (Figure 6).

3. Complete the additional rings in the same manner. To cover the 5½-inch-diameter ring, cut a 6¼ × 30-inch fabric strip; for the 7-inch-diameter ring, work with a 6¼ × 45-inch strip.

4. Layer the burlap rings and fantail back as directed in Making Fabric Ruffles directions. Sew or glue the turkey body on top of the ruffled feather rings.

My Favorite Apron, Turkey Style

Approximate size:
Fits an average adult man
or woman

MATERIALS NEEDED:
1 yard of holiday print fabric for
    apron
Scraps of coordinating fabrics
    for appliqué
Paper-backed fusible webbing
2 inches of red crinkled or
    gathered ribbon
Brown embroidery floss
Fabric paint
Beads for eyes (optional)

1. Referring to the patterns and instructions in Chapter 3, make My Favorite Apron from a suitable holiday print fabric.

2. Because the feather print used for this apron is so busy, we chose a subtle print to make the entire tail-feather appliqué instead of different fabrics for each layer of feathers. Trace the turkey tail and body patterns (page 160) onto the paper backing of the fusible webbing. Rough-cut these pieces and fuse them onto the appropriate fabrics. Cut out the fused pieces on the traced lines, then fuse them in place on the apron front.

3. Trace the feather detail lines onto the tail. Following the manufacturer's directions, practice with the fabric paint on a scrap first; then trace the detail lines and outside edges of the tail and body with paint.

4. Fuse two small scraps of yellow fabric wrong sides together. Cut the turkey's beak from this fused fabric. Embroider the beak opening with brown floss.

5. Secure a 2-inch-long piece of crinkled ribbon to the back side of the beak to make the wattle. (Secure the loose end of the ribbon so the crinkles won't come out.) Fuse or stitch the beak in place on the turkey's head. Add beads or paint for eyes.

I Love Turkey Pillow

Approximate size:
18 inches

MATERIALS NEEDED:
½ yard of fabric for the pillow
    top and back
½ yard of fabric for ruffle
Scraps for appliqué
Paper-backed fusible webbing
Thermore™ or fleece
Polyester filling

This pillow was truly created as a scrap project. The appliqué was originally made for the apron, but the prints were too busy to work well together. Since my policy is "never throw anything away," I created a pillow. It is called "I Love Turkey," not to be misinterpreted as "I Love A Turkey," lest my husband be offended!

1. Using the Shirred Heart Pillow pattern on pages 90 and 91, cut one pillow front and one pillow back. Cut two more hearts of fleece. Baste a fleece heart to the wrong side of each fabric heart.

2. Trace the turkey tail and body patterns (page 160) onto the paper backing of the fusible webbing. Rough-cut these pieces and fuse them onto the appropriate fabrics. Cut out the fused pieces on the traced lines, then fuse them in place on the pillow front. Trace feather detail lines on the tail.

3. Machine-stitch a narrow zigzag satin-stitch on the feather detail lines and around the outside edges of feathers and body.

4. Cut and piece strips to make a 7½ × 78-inch strip for the ruffle. Referring to the ruffle instructions on pages 61–63, make a 3¼-inch finished-size ruffle.

5. See Pillow Finishing on page 65 for directions on putting the pillow together.

6. Complete the turkey beak, wattle, and eyes as for the apron appliqué. Use glue to attach the beak and wattle to the turkey head.

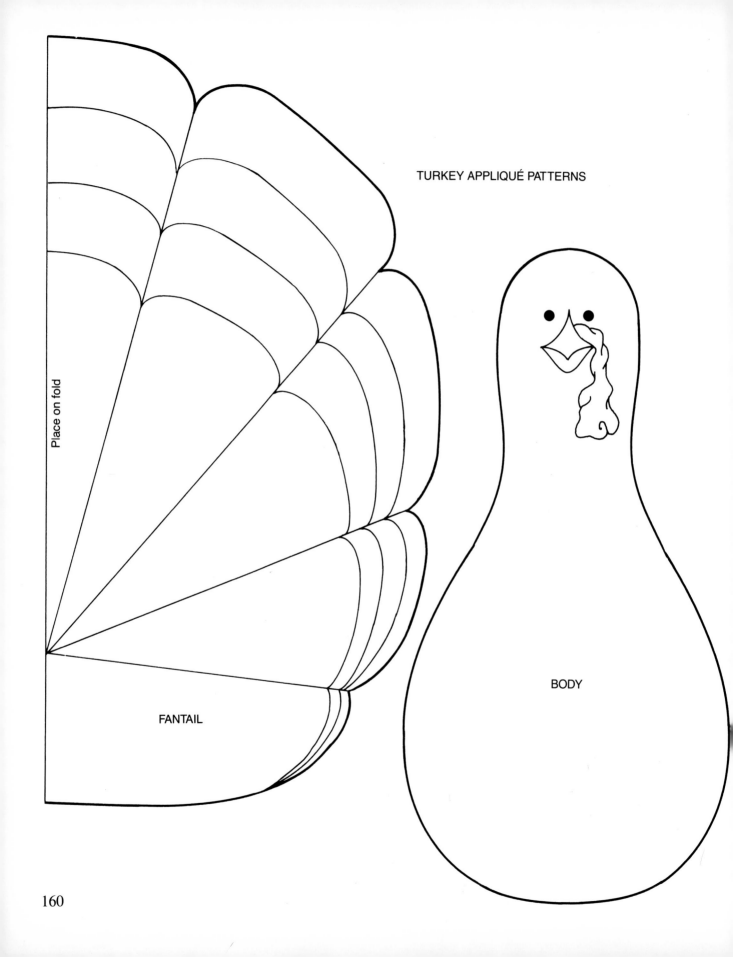

TURKEY APPLIQUÉ PATTERNS

Place on fold

FANTAIL

BODY

160

CHAPTER TWELVE

THE CELEBRATION VEST

This vest is especially designed for people who like to accomplish a lot at one time. Make one vest and wear it on every holiday. In addition, this item could be personalized to include your birthday and other events that you celebrate.

You can use any vest pattern you have as long as it doesn't have darts, or enlarge the pattern on page 166. Either way it is a good idea to start off by making a muslin version that you can check for fit. You can make your vest with lightweight batting added or it can be unquilted.

String Quilting

String quilting, or string piecing, is my favorite way to use scraps. It is the traditional name for the technique of using assorted narrow strips of fabrics in quilt pieces. Stitch and flip, a phrase used today, is a more explicit description of the technique. It is a fascinating way to use even the smallest pieces of fabric. If you don't have small scraps of fabric, you can cut them from what you have. They can be straight, parallel strips of the same width, or parallel strips of random widths, or irregular. I usually prefer irregular strips and often include other irregular shapes.

Most people prefer string quilting on a base material. This may be easier to understand when you read the instructions for a specific project.

Base Material Possibilities

Papers

Any kind of paper used as a base material must be torn away eventually, but not until the piecing is complete. The crispness of paper makes the piecing easy and accurate. It also stabilizes bias edges. It is a good idea, however, to test the ease of tearing before many strips are stitched. If the paper does not pull away easily, use a smaller stitch. As the needle punches through more closely it will perforate the paper for easier removal.

Be prepared to change needles on the sewing machine more often if you use a paper base for string quilting. Paper seems to dull needles just as it dulls scissors. The signals of a dull needle are skipped stitches, loud stitches, and pulled threads.

Newspaper was the traditional material of quiltmakers in the 19th and early 20th centuries because it was readily available. It was a perfect example of recycling before anyone knew the word. Newspaper is still the least expensive material, but I don't like to use it because the ink tends to rub off on my hands and eventually transfers to the fabric.

Brown grocery bags are usually too thick to tear away easily after stitching.

Freezer paper is my favorite. When using freezer paper, place the waxy side next to the fabric. This holds the fabric closest to it in place without pins, just press lightly.

Fabric

Muslin, as the base material, remains a permanent part of the project. Please preshrink muslin. The quality of available muslins varies and severe shrinkage after the string quilting is completed would be disastrous.

Tear-away background stabilizer is classified as a nonwoven fabric, but it is often used for string quilting because it can be torn away from stitched areas. It must be torn carefully to prevent stretching.

Quilt-as-You-Sew Variation

If you layer fleece or Thermore™ on top of a muslin base and string-piece through both layers, the quilting is done when the piecing is done! This type of vest, however, doesn't necessarily need to be quilted.

Making the Vest Sections

Select an assortment of holiday scraps you want to work with. Have a general plan for how you want to position each holiday. Consider whether you want to give extra emphasis to one holiday or if you want to include other, more personal, celebrations. Figure 1 is a general guide for the vest as pictured. The fabrics you choose, the holidays or events you want to emphasize, and personal choice will dictate your decisions.

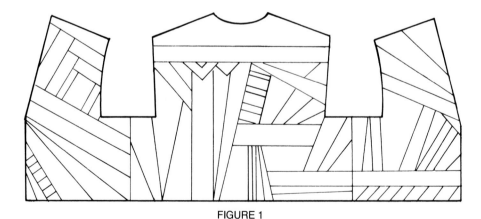

FIGURE 1

1. Cut full-size vest fronts and a back from your base material. If you are using disposable or removable base material (tear-away stabilizer, freezer paper, or paper), cut those pieces the *finished size* of the vest sections. Seam allowances will be added when trimming scraps. Base material is much

164

easier to tear away when it isn't caught in the garment's seams. If you are using a fabric base that will not be removed, then you should include seam allowances in the cut size.

2. Select your first two strips of scraps. Position them anywhere on the base material with right sides together. Machine-stitch along the edge of the two strips (Figure 2). It is very important for the stitching line to be straight; curves in the stitching will prevent the strips from laying flat. For now, let the ends of the scraps hang off the edge of the base—these will form the seam allowance, but trimming comes later.

3. Flip the strip just stitched to the right side and press it flat (Figure 3).

4. Place the next strip facedown along one raw edge of the patchwork and stitch again (Figure 4). Stitch and flip as often as necessary to fill the base material with patchwork. This will be determined both by the size of the base piece and the width of the scraps. Note: Irregular strips tend to radiate from a point if all the narrow ends are on the same side of the base. This is sometimes very effective, but if you want to prevent that, then alternate the placement of the narrow ends (Figure 5).

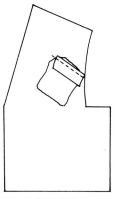

FIGURE 2

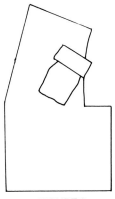

FIGURE 3

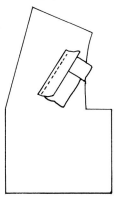

FIGURE 4

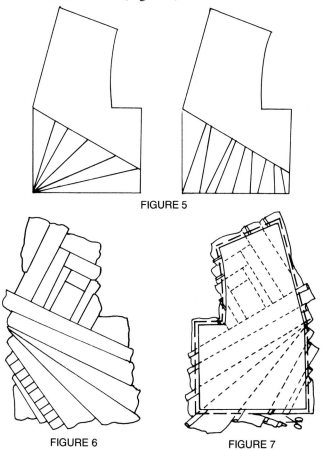

FIGURE 5

FIGURE 6 FIGURE 7

5. When the surface of the base material is covered (Figure 6), it is time to trim away the excess scrap fabric. If you used removable base material, this is when you create the seam allowances (Figure 7).

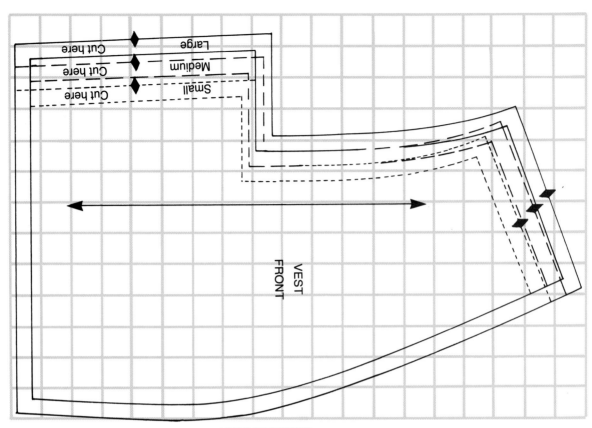

Cut here — Large
Cut here — Medium
Cut here — Small

VEST
FRONT

VEST PATTERNS

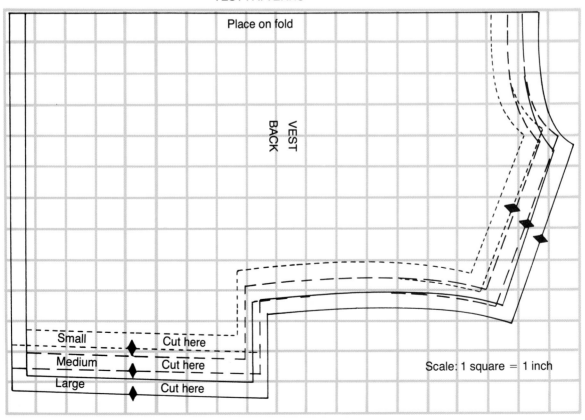

Place on fold

VEST
BACK

Small	Cut here
Medium	Cut here
Large	Cut here

Scale: 1 square = 1 inch

This is contrary to the old days, when it seems that the base material (which was often newspaper) was either sewn into the seam allowances or removed before the process of joining pieces. To remove the base material now eliminates the benefit of stability and increases the risk of stretching the remaining fabric. Sewing the base material into the seams makes it much more difficult to remove.

Finishing the Vest

The vest shown is finished in a nontraditional manner, with button (and bell!) and loop closures at the shoulders. There is a strip of light-colored fabric string-quilted across the width of the vest back. This strip creates the illusion of a yoke, and provides the perfect place to write a personal message with fabric paint. I added prairie points (dimensional fabric triangles) to the bottom of this strip on the left side (see photo on pages 162 and 163).

1. To make a prairie point, begin with a square of fabric 1½ times larger than the desired finished *width*. Fold the square in half diagonally to make a triangle. Fold again to create a smaller triangle (Figure 8). All the raw edges will be on one side.

2. Make as many prairie points as desired. Different sizes of prairie points can be stacked for special effect. Position prairie points on the vest and tack them in place.

3. Stitch the string-quilted vest fronts and back together at the side seams.

4. Cut two vest fronts and one back from both the lining fabric and the batting. Sew the lining pieces together at the side seams, then stitch the batting pieces together in the same manner. Trim the batting seam allowances.

5. Layer the vest top, lining, and batting. The fabric pieces should be right sides together, and the batting should be against the *wrong* side of the vest lining. Match all side seams carefully.

6. Stitch all the layers together along the outside edges, leaving the shoulder seams open (Figure 9).

7. If you used a removable base material, now is the time to remove it. Tear it away carefully, being sure not to pull out the stitching.

8. Turn the vest right side out through the openings at the shoulders. Turn the shoulder seam allowances to the inside.

9. Don't make the button (or bell) loops individually. Instead, position the ends of an 8-inch length of cording on each side of the open seam (Figure 10), and adjust loops for the correct size. Tack these loops in position, then slip-stitch the shoulder seams closed.

10. Topstitch around the entire outside edges of the vest. Quilt as desired.

11. Sew buttons and/or bells onto the vest front at the shoulders, aligning them with the loops on the back shoulders.

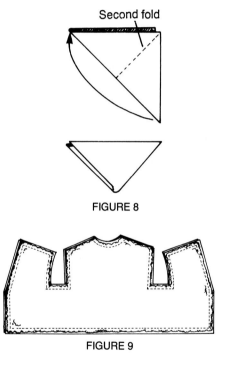

Second fold

FIGURE 8

FIGURE 9

FIGURE 10

167

INDEX

Recommended Products

Products come and go, so their availability cannot be guaranteed for the life of this book. Most products named in this book are available at sewing and craft stores. The following products, however, are unique and justify special mention.

Country Wire Quilt Hangers. Look for these hangers at quilting and craft stores, in mail order catalogs, or write to Country Wire, 3525 Broad Street, Chamblee, GA 30366.

Thermore™. A low-loft, nonbearding batting available at fabric and quilting stores, or write to Hobbs Bonded Fibers, Craft Product Div., South McKinney Street, Mexia, TX 76667.

Pigma™ Pens. These indelible markers come in a variety of fine points and colors and are ideal for cloth doll facial features and signature quilts. Look for them in art and craft stores, mail order catalogs, or write to Sakura of America, 30470 Whipple Road, Union City, CA 94587.

All of us at Meredith® Press are dedicated to offering you, our customer, the best books we can create. We are particularly concerned that instructions for making projects are clear and accurate. Please address correspondence to Customer Service Department, Meredith® Press, 150 E. 52nd Street, New York, NY 10022, or call 1-800-678-2665.